HOOFING IT!

A WALKING GUIDE  NGS

Presented by

SARATOGA SPRINGS PRESERVATION FOUNDATION

Copyright © 2005 by Saratoga Springs Preservation Foundation
ISBN: 0-9770803-0-7
This book was designed and prepared for publication by
Margaret Craig of PingPong Graphics www.pingponginc.com
Photo Postproduction by Granite Studios, LLC www.granitestudios.com
Printing by GM Printing, New York, NY

To order from the publisher:
SARATOGA SPRINGS PRESERVATION FOUNDATION
P.O. Box 442
117 Grand Avenue
Saratoga Springs, New York 12866
(518) 518-587-5030
http://www.saratogapreservation.org

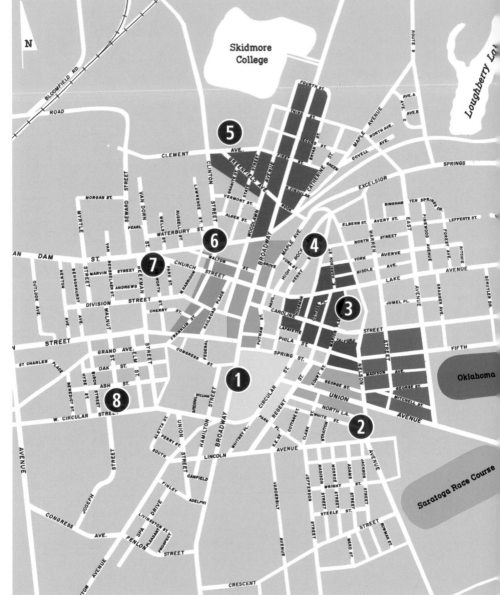

Skidmore College

N

SARATOGA SPRINGS NEIGHBORHOODS

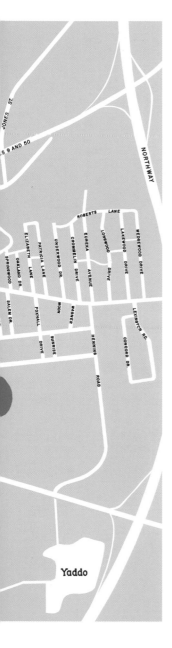

Written by Carrie Woerner, Executive Director
Saratoga Springs Preservation Foundation

Photography by Mark W. Beckerman

Book Design by Margaret Craig, PingPong Graphics

TABLE OF CONTENTS

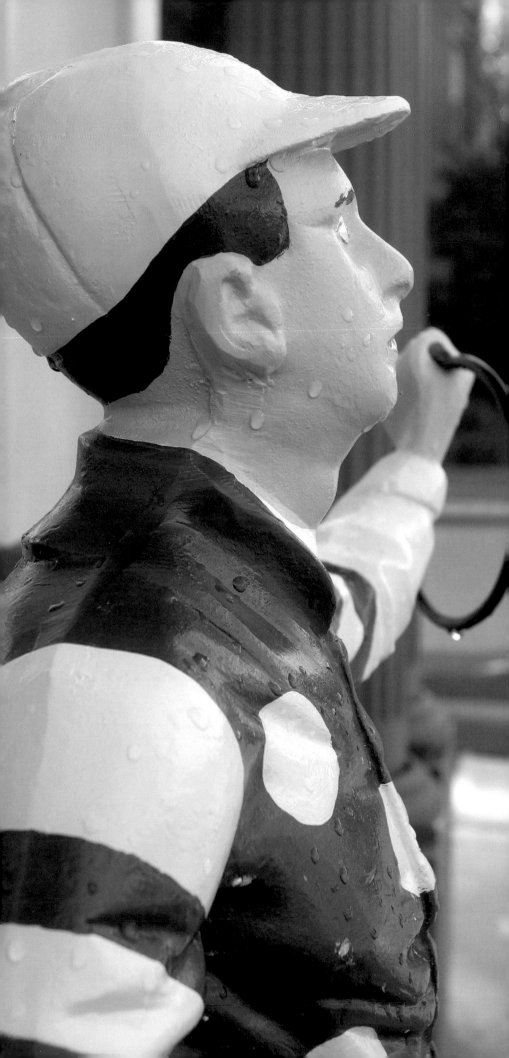

INTRODUCTION
and
ACKNOWLEDGEMENTS

Learning to look is a pleasure;
the buildings will embrace your eyes.

Judith Lynch Waldhorn - Author, Researcher, Authority on Victorian Architecture

*W*hile we may be biased, we think that there is nothing finer than a stroll through one of the historic neighborhoods in Saratoga Springs. The variety of shapes and patterns in the architecture sets up a complex and varied rhythm that creates an excitement all its own. As you meander along the tree-lined streets, you'll find yourself in a veritable painter's palette of color. From the strong, restrained white Greek Revivals in Franklin Square, to the extroverted, playful pastels of the Queen Anne houses of Union Avenue, Saratoga Springs is a feast for the eyes.

The history of Saratoga Springs is laid out for you as you walk through its streets. Each house, each building, each piece of sculpture tells its own story of the time when it was created and the people who created it. Look closely at the details of each building and you can find stylistic influences of far-flung cultures. In the architecture, you can sense how the people of this very American city adopted and claimed those styles for their own.

We've developed and written *Hoofing It!* to be the tour guide you always wanted. You'll find the book organized into eight separate walking tours that correspond to the city's various historic neighborhoods. The tours are illustrated with luminous color photographs. We've highlighted the architecture and history behind a few of the buildings along the way — some are magnificent reminders of Saratoga's history as a resort destination, others are testaments to the individuals who worked to build the city. Taken together they are a living museum of the history and art that is Saratoga Springs.

Much of the content of *Hoofing It!* comes from the history files and building inventory sheets that have been maintained by the Saratoga Springs Preservation Foundation since the mid-1970s. This guide would not have been possible without the work of scores of Preservation Foundation staff and volunteers who, over the last 30 years have researched the history and architecture of houses across the city. We would especially like to thank James Kettlewell, who is truly the dean of Saratoga Springs' architectural history, Beatrice Sweeney, Julia Stokes, Martha Stonequist, Field Horne, Sonia Taub, and Douglas Kerr. They and many others have always given generously of their time and talents over the years, and we hope this book does justice to their work.

Dr. Mark Beckerman's brilliant photographs capture the sights of Saratoga Springs. Through his eyes we see Saratoga Springs anew. His images show us a city full of color and light. With his gift of the Beckerman Archive, Dr. Beckerman has given the Preservation Foundation and the citizens of Saratoga Springs a remarkable resource for generations to come. We are deeply grateful to be the recipient of this body of work.

Margie Craig is the amazingly talented designer who took our notion for a walking tour guide and turned it into the book you are now holding. Margie has been a wonderful creative partner throughout the project. Kathie Zilahy took on the challenge to compile all of the information and wrote the first draft. Jim Hill of Redspring Communication offered invaluable encouragement and guidance as we embarked on this project. Holly Schwarz-Lawton and Penny Ruhm of Saratoga On the Move (an affiliate of America On the Move) and Betsey Sutton calibrated the various tour routes.

Susan Milner, Field Horne, Holly Schwarz-Lawton, Dr. Nancy Roberts, Karen Christensen, Katy Stenhouse, James Kettlewell and others critiqued various versions. Mary Caroline Powers offered her services as an editor, and the book is better for her tremendous assistance. Any remaining errors of fact or style are entirely ours.

Several individuals and firms offered generous financial support to create *Hoofing It!*. We would like to thank Prudential Manor Homes, members of the Fox family--Norman, Harvey and Kassie, Realty USA, Roohan Realty, Gallery 100, Barbara Glaser, Ed Woerner, and 70 Beekman Street Fine Art Gallery for underwriting this project.

Finally, we would like to thank all of the members of the 2004-2005 Board of Directors of the Preservation Foundation for their support, and especially to James Rossi of XPO Enterprises, for his creativity in conceiving this project and his leadership in the development of *Hoofing It!* and to Susan Svoboda, George Hathaway and Mark Lawton for their dedication to bringing the book to market.

We hope you enjoy *Hoofing It!* around our beautiful city. It's a great day for a walk.

1 The Visitor Center 297 Broadway

MARK BECKERMAN

𝔐ark Beckerman is a documentary photographer and filmmaker. As a photojournalist he has traveled widely and his work seems to resemble scenes from motion pictures. Beckerman's images of Saratoga Springs have a clarity and accuracy of color that reveal details and patterns in the architecture. His work is painterly, drawing the viewer into the frame. Beckerman's work on the Beckerman Archive is reminiscent of the Hudson River School. Over 200 of his images illustrate *Hoofing It!*.

Born in 1945 in Brooklyn, Beckerman showed serious interest in photography by age 10. In his late teens, looking for a career in show business, Beckerman started in the mailroom at Embassy Pictures. Within a few weeks, the head of public relations at Embassy recruited the young Beckerman. One evening, while working at a press event for Embassy, he bumped into Salvadore Dali on the street and brought Dali inside to meet the head of Embassy, Joseph E. Levine. The astonished movie mogul slapped Beckerman on the back and said, "Stick with me kid, I'll make a helluva press agent out of you." Beckerman's early exposure to filmmaking influenced his later photographic work.

At 22, Beckerman graduated from a professional photography program in New York City, and went to work at the *New York Daily News*. Working at night in Manhattan, covering breaking news, Mark was befriended by renowned film noir photographer Weegee (Arthur Felig) and syndicated columnist Walter Winchell. Beckerman's early newspaper work shows these influences. He also had in the staff of the *Daily News* great teachers — 55 of the best picture makers in the world, many of whom were Pulitzer Prize winners.

In 1968, Beckerman enrolled in photography courses at The New School, studying under the celebrated German photographer, Joseph Breitenbach. The course, "Photography as Art," became the pivotal moment in his artistic development. Shortly after completing the course and under the strong influence of Breitenbach, Beckerman's fine art picture of Central Park in the snow appeared in the centerfold

Union Ave.

of the *Daily News* and was seen that day by 4 million people.

After that Beckerman began to receive many special assignments to provide photo illustrations for feature stories. The newspaper sent the 23-year old artist back to school to learn the "miniature" 35mm techniques and equipment that were beginning to replace the big, bulky press cameras and were changing photojournalism. Beckerman was one of the first six *News* photographers to be trained in this new technology. Encouragement came from unexpected places. The chief photographer at the time, John Duprey, took Beckerman aside and told him, "Stick with what you're doing. Don't let people try to change you. And don't worry."

One highlight of this time in his career was a 1967 three-part story on the gentrification of the Upper West Side of Manhattan. The photographs for the story appear again in a gallery show in 2005 in Manhattan. While at the *Daily News*, Beckerman photographed three U.S. presidents and traveled with Nelson Rockefeller on the gubernatorial campaign trail. His pictures have appeared in television advertisements, magazines, all of the New York City newspapers, print advertising campaigns and college catalogues.

In the late 1960s, Beckerman was on the front lines of the Martin Luther King riots in Harlem, Newark and Plainfield, New Jersey, where he experienced first-hand the increasing violence in the urban core. While his artistic drive never waned, he began to rethink his career choices and returned to another childhood dream. So, in 1972, Beckerman became a veterinarian in order to aid animals.

During his 25-year career as a vet, which started in Saratoga Springs working for equine veterinarian Dr. Steven Lascher, Beckerman became the first two-term president of the Long Island Veterinary Medical Society. He also served on the New York State Veterinary Medical Society Board of Directors. Even while building his own practice, Beckerman continued to produce images; his pictures have served as teaching tools and historic documentation for the Veterinary Medical Society. Beckerman's work during this time was also featured on the cover of *Veterinary Medicine*, a professional journal.

In 2000, Beckerman sold his practice and retired. He journeyed to China, Cuba, the Galapagos, as well as many countries in Europe.

He built a state of the art darkroom to produce fine art prints. And then, photography went digital. And just as he was once on the forefront of 35mm technology, Beckerman joined the vanguard of fine art digital photographers. His recent work has appeared in journals, film and ad campaigns. The 5,000 image Beckerman Archive is principally digital and served as the creative force behind *Hoofing It!*.

In retrospect, his early experience in documenting neighborhood development shaped Beckerman's later drive to be actively involved in his community and in social interest groups. He has served on the board of the Borough of Manhattan Community College. He is also on the Board of the Anderson Ranch Arts Center in Aspen, Colorado. And here in Saratoga Springs, Beckerman is a member of the national advisory board of the Tang Teaching Museum. His photographs are in many private collections.

Married to Susan, a graduate and current trustee of Skidmore College, they live in the middle of Mark's story on the Upper West Side of Manhattan. Mark and Susan met while in high school and married 35 years later – it's a long story! The Beckermans also have a home in Snowmass Village, Colorado.

In June 2005, Beckerman will begin work on a new book. During a 2,500-mile solo motorcycle expedition across the United States, he plans to document the vacant and decaying structures from defunct economies. He will visit forgotten scenic zones and meet the people who live in these parts of America.

{ ARTIST STATEMENT }

"Working in Saratoga Springs was like an artist's dream to be dropped into the palette. Like Alice, I was made small and Saratoga became a painter's palette of color. The city kept motivating me to seek more colors and patterns. So I would work from 6 a.m. to catch the early light and colors to evening when the artificial light of Caroline Street and the carousel created the mystery and dimension that I learned from Weegee back in the 1960s.

The other part that was a great joy – by the fifth or sixth day, people would stop me on Broadway and say 'Aren't you the guy we saw on the ladder on Union Avenue?' They would share with me another anecdote and show me other places to shoot. That's what I liked about this job."

MARK BECKERMAN   15

1 Hathorn Spring

The city of Saratoga Springs, population 26,186, is in central Saratoga County. Located at the southeast edge of the Adirondack Mountains, it lies on a geological fault from which issue numerous mineral springs. High Rock Spring, first described by Sir William Johnson in 1771, began to attract health seekers, and in 1783 Philip Schuyler cut a 10 mile (16 km) path from the present Schuylerville. Primitive lodgings were built, and in 1802 Gideon Putnam opened Union Hall, a three-story hotel near Congress Spring, and platted a village along a broad main street. In 1811 Putnam began another hotel, Congress Hall, and competitors erected the Columbian (1809), Pavilion (1819), and United States (1824) Hotels. The Town of Saratoga Springs was formed in 1819 from the Town of Saratoga. John Clarke, a New York City entrepreneur, bought Congress Spring in 1823 and marketed its water throughout the country and abroad. Beginning in 1829 he began development of Congress Park as an exercise ground for those who took water at the spring.

The availability of inexpensive steamship service on the Hudson in the 1820s and the completion of the Erie Canal in 1825 made Saratoga Springs a feature of the Fashionable Tour. The increasingly urban center of the town was incorporated as a village in 1826. The Saratoga and Schenectady Railroad (1832-33), the second in New York State, greatly enhanced its accessibility. Close to 50,000 visitors a year visited antebellum Saratoga Springs. The village was especially popular with southerners fleeing their plantations in the summer. At Saratoga Springs they encountered free African American workers in substantial numbers (3-4% of the village's summer population). The seasonal, service-based economy also provided work for Irish immigrants and for women. The hotels grew ever larger, with enormous public spaces: parlors, dining rooms, and verandas. While some visitors came purely for therapeutic purposes, Saratoga Springs drew the curious and, increasingly, pleasure seekers. In consequence, dances and amusements became central to its image early on, gambling was introduced by 1835, and sporting events developed gradually beginning with harness racing in 1847.

The Civil War cut Saratoga Springs off from its southern clientele,

Inside the Casino

Grand Union Garden Party

but under the influence of sportsman John Morrissey, the resort entered into an even greater period of prosperity and fame. Morrissey opened a gaming house in 1862 and joined with three New York City turfmen to offer a thoroughbred race meeting the following year. It was a great success, and in 1864 they began development of the present Saratoga Race Course, the oldest horse-racing venue in the United States, and launched the Travers Stakes, America's oldest stakes race. The racetrack's thriving condition enabled Morrissey to expand his operations; he bought land adjacent to Congress Park and built the Italianate Club House (1870-71), a gambling casino. Department store magnate A. T. Stewart bought Union Hall in 1872 and remodeled it on a luxurious scale as the Grand Union Hotel. Congress Hall and the United States Hotel were also rebuilt, the latter in 1872-74 with 768 rooms, a dining room of more than 10,000 sq. ft. (930 sq. m.), a half mile (0.8 km) of verandas, and 1,000 rocking chairs. No American resort could present such a conglomeration of hostelries; among them, the three largest hotels could accommodate 5,000 guests. Visitors to Saratoga Springs could browse in attractive shops, visit an Indian encampment, attend a circus, hire rigs for pleasure drives, or patronize bowling alleys or shooting galleries. In 1875, 1876 and 1879, Morrissey promoted rowing meets on Saratoga Lake, and the first such regatta was one of the most newsworthy events of its day. Politicians and generals continued to visit the springs; in 1885 Ulysses Grant, dying of cancer, came to Mt. McGregor, 8 miles (13 km) north of Saratoga Springs, to finish his memoirs.

In 1893 Richard Canfield bought the Club House, renamed it the Casino and, in 1902, added a spectacular dining room. Despite national economic recession, the 1890s was one of the most glittering periods for Saratoga Springs, but the era came to the end when the Casino closed in 1907 and the state Legislature passed the Agnew-Hart Bill, which prevented race wagering in 1911 and 1912. Both tourism and industry benefited from the construction of two additional railroad lines. The Adirondack Railroad (1865-71, later Delaware and Hudson) connected Saratoga Springs to the central Adirondacks; the Saratoga Lake Railroad (1881-82) provided connections to Boston. The Saratoga line was built largely by Italian laborers, and those who remained in the area were the start of a thriving Italian neighborhood on the West Side. Some industrial

Early Regatta on Saratoga Lake   A Day at the Races

development also began. While inconsequential alongside the tourist
industry, it provided year-round employment. Chief among the firms
were G. F. Harvey Co. (pharmaceuticals) and Baker and Shevlin
(metal castings). Clark Textile Co. began producing gloves in 1906;
its successors, the Van Raalte Co. (1919) and Saratoga Knitting Mill
(1975), produced knit goods until 1986.

Saratoga Springs waters retained their popularity throughout the
19th century and became even more valuable when, in the 1880s, a
method was devised to extract carbonic gas from them to carbonate
bottled beverages. Gas companies, seeking greater profits, pumped
more than 150 million gallons (568,000 l) of spring water, and
the aquifer's water level dropped almost 100 feet (30 m). In 1908,
the state legislature passed an antipumping act (upheld by the
U.S. Supreme Court in 1911), and beginning in 1909, New York
State acquired more than 100 springs to prevent their commercial
exploitation and consequent destruction. Modest bathhouse
development by the state soon followed. An elaborate new resort and
therapy complex opened in 1935, funded in part by federal money
from the Reconstruction Finance Corp., but never succeeded in
rivaling the great European spas or the village's 19th-century heyday.
Saratoga Springs, incorporated as a city in 1915, seemed to be in
decline, but the race course had reopened in 1913 and maintained
a high standard of racing. Although the Casino had closed, other
gambling houses opened, mostly along Saratoga Lake, within city
limits but 3.5 miles (5.6 km) from the city center. Boxers such as Jack
Dempsey and Gene Tunney followed, and the city retained its raffish
reputation from its association with the sporting life. Yet, Yaddo
(1893), a mansion with gardens, opened in 1926 as a retreat for
writers, artists and composers.

The growth of automobile touring after World War I undercut the
custom of an extended vacation in one place; visitors to Saratoga
Springs complained of outmoded sanitary facilities, badly ventilated
rooms, and the idleness of traditional hotel life. A Jewish clientele
expanded substantially in the new century as immigrant families
acquired the time and money for vacations, but hotel owners
converted only small and midsized hotels for their use; the United
States Hotel was razed in 1945-46, and the Grand Union followed in
1952-53. In 1951, following police raids and extensive publicity from

Grandstand Seats - Saratoga Race Course

the Kefauver Commission, authorities ended public gambling. Much distinguished architecture was allowed to fall into ruin. Just when it seemed the city might go altogether to seed, however, the Northway was built though Saratoga Springs (1963). The 5,100-seat Saratoga Performing Arts Center (SPAC) opened in 1966, offering both classical and popular entertainment. Skidmore College's expansion on a new campus from 1963 to 1971 increased its economic impact on the city and helped prepare Saratoga Springs for the historic preservation movement, which began locally in 1977 and restored the Spa City's attractiveness to tourists and new residents.

Saratoga's race track survived all the ups and downs; daily track attendance in the 1990s exceeded 20,000 horseplayers for an enlarged six-week season, and events such as the Fasig-Tipton yearling auction and the annual National Thoroughbred Racing Hall of Fame induction ceremony continue to dominate the summer calendar. Saratoga's reputation as a distinctive American cultural expression has been disseminated in such disparate works as Edith Wharton's unfinished *The Buccaneers* (1938), Edna Ferber's *Saratoga Trunk* (1941), and E. L. Doctorow's *Billy Bathgate* (1989). Beginning with the 1959 opening of an industrial park, the city has sought to diversify its economy. Major manufacturers in 2003 included Stewart's Ice Cream Co., Quad/Graphics (printing), Ball Metal Container Group, Espey Manufacturing and Electronics Corp., and Ellsworth Ice Cream Co. Saratoga Springs is a bedroom community for Albany, and benefits from the presence of Skidmore College (1903), Empire State College (1971), and many museums, including the National Museum of Racing (1950), the National Museum of Dance (1986), and the New York State Military Museum (2002). Its permanent population increased almost 40% between 1960 and 2000. Summer tourism, however, continues to be its bread and butter, augmented by a thriving year-round convention business.

From Peter Eisenstadt, ed., The Encyclopedia of New York State (Syracuse: Syracuse University Press, 2005). © 2005 by Syracuse University Press. Reprinted by permission of the publisher.

1722 North Broadway, S. Gifford Slocum

Saratoga Springs has a long architectural tradition of exceptional design. Splendid hotels, exuberant, extroverted residences, and commanding public and commercial buildings are all the product of the talented architects who have practiced their art in Saratoga Springs. Highlighted here are but a few of the many designers who were attracted to the city in the 19th century.

R. Newton Brezee

R. Newton Brezee practiced architecture in Saratoga Springs for 45 years, leaving behind a significant legacy of residential and public buildings. Forty-nine buildings in all have been identified in the city as having been designed by Brezee.

Brezee moved to Saratoga Springs at the age of 21, and for his first five years in residence, he worked as a carpenter. In 1877, Brezee left Saratoga Springs for Garden City, New York, where he spent the next eight years working for the A. T. Stewart estate. Alexander Tunney Stewart was the wealthy owner of the world's largest retail store in New York City, A.T. Stewart and Co. For Saratogians, Stewart was better known for having invested over $1 million dollars to acquire and modernize the Union Hotel, which re-opened in 1874 as the Grand Union Hotel. During this same time period, Stewart began an ambitious project to develop a planned community on land he owned on Long Island; this planned village was to be known as Garden City. Unfortunately, Stewart died before he could see his vision realized.

The Garden City project went forward under the direction of Stewart's trusted friend, Henry Hilton. It is likely that while working on it Brezee gained the skills and experience for his future career. Brezee returned to Saratoga Springs in 1884 and established a contracting and building firm with a partner, Oscar C. Moody. The partnership did not last a full year, and by September 1884 Brezee had opened his own office, advertising himself as "Architect and Building Superintendent."

Brezee's announcement came at an opportune time. There was a building boom underway in Saratoga Springs, and his skills as both a designer and a builder were in demand. Despite having no formal training in architecture, Brezee became one of the city's leading architects. He maintained an office at 432 Broadway for more than 40 years and over the years designed some of the most prestigious houses in the city. Based on the designs of the houses he built, Brezee's style appears to have been most heavily influenced by the Queen Anne and Richardsonian Romanesque forms.

Gilbert Croff

Gilbert Croff, a native of Vermont, arrived in Saratoga Springs in about 1869, possibly coming from Fort Edward, New York. Croff was a published architect and lived and worked in Saratoga Springs until 1899, when he moved to New York City. Most notable for his Second Empire style residences, Croff designed several major commercial buildings in the city, including the Ainsworth Building on Broadway. He is the author of *Model Suburban Architecture* (1870) and *Progressive American Architecture* (1875). His own residence in Saratoga Springs, which was located on the corner of Broadway and Lincoln Avenue, appeared in *Architect and Building Monthly*, Vol 1., January 1871, page 168. He not only designed in Saratoga Springs and the immediate vicinity, but also has works attributed to him in Vermont, Massachusetts, Pennsylvania, Ohio and Canada.

S.Gifford Slocum

Samuel Gifford Slocum opened his architecture practice in Saratoga in 1882 with an office at 440 Broadway. An advertisement in a guidebook in 1887 listed 13 of Slocum's "most recent" works in Saratoga Springs. The guidebook cited country houses as a specialty, although a number of prominent commercial and public buildings in Saratoga Springs were designed by Slocum. In 1889, Slocum moved to Philadelphia where he set up his permanent headquarters. *The Saratogian* newspaper reported in June 1888 that Slocum intended to "maintain a branch office in Saratoga Springs where he has for the past seven years met with such substantial marks of appreciation."

Many of Slocum's buildings are still in use, including the Annandale Mansion on Clinton Street, Redstone Villa at 795 Broadway and the Moriarta building at 511 Broadway, and provide excellent examples of the Queen Anne and Richardsonian Romansque styles. Slocum had at least one published design; the residence of H.S. Leech, at 2 Union Ave. (then 54 Circular St.), appeared in the March 1889 issue of the *Inland Architect and News Record*. Unfortunately, this building is no longer standing.

15 Fifth Ave., Gilbert Croff

Croff Design, Saratoga Springs

153 Regent St., William Vaughan

Frelin G. Vaughan

Frelin Vaughan began his practice of architecture in Saratoga Springs in partnership with John D. Stevens in 1872. From their offices at 162 Broadway, the partners designed the magnificent United States Hotel in 1874. The partnership ended in the late 1870s, when Stevens moved to New York City. Frelin Vaughan continued to work in Saratoga Springs designing both residences and commercial structures. Among the buildings designed by him that are still in existence are the YMCA building at 437 Broadway, the house at 24 Circular St., and the row houses on Thomas Street.

William Vaughan

Grandson of Frelin Vaughan, William Vaughan set up his architectural practice in 1919 with an office at 400 Broadway. Vaughan began his career with William Case and Son, Contractors, where his father had been a foreman for 15 years. The younger Vaughan spent four years as a laborer then two years as a draftsman. In the mid-1920s, he assumed the distinction of "local architect" after the firm of Brezee and Mallory dissolved in 1926, being the only architect listed in the city directories. Vaughan's designs would most closely be classified as Colonial Revival with a number of residential, vernacular houses to his credit as well.

Sources:
Saratoga Springs City Historian Files, and Burns, Kathryn A. An Inventory and Analysis of the Work of Architect R. Newton Brezee, Saratoga Springs, N.Y. (1884-1929). Washington D.C. 1980.

124 Circular St., Frelin Vaughan

CONGRESS PARK

1 Congress Park Carousel

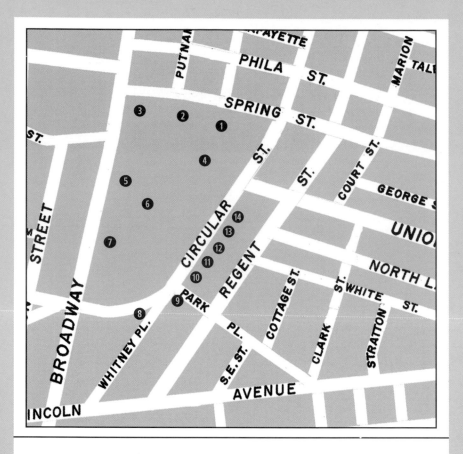

TOUR DETAILS
Distance: 1.2 miles
Steps: 2,353
Time: Approximately 30 minutes
Terrain: Slightly hilly, some uneven surfaces
Directions: Enter at Spring St. near Henry St., around the Italian Gardens, up to Spirit of Life, over to Casino, on to Trask Steps, exit onto W. Circular St. Follow Circular St. past the Batchellor Mansion, north to Spring St. West on Spring St. to the park entrance.

TOUR HIGHLIGHTS

❶ Italian Gardens
❷ Carousel
❸ "The Spirit of Life" Statue
❹ Canfield Casino
❺ Congress Spring Pavilion
❻ Columbian Spring Pavilion
❼ Katrina Trask Memorial Staircase

❽ 20 Circular St.
❾ 24 Circular St.
❿ 30 Circular St.
⓫ 34 Circular St.
⓬ 38 Circular St.
⓭ 42 Circular St.
⓮ 46 Circular St.

CONGRESS PARK

W hen we look at the manicured lawns and graceful hillsides
of Congress Park today, it is hard to imagine that in 1802, when
Gideon Putnam encountered this land, it was little more than a
swamp.

The Congress Spring itself had been discovered in 1792 by Nicholas
Gilman, a member of the first United States Congress from Vermont.
The name of the spring reflects Gilman's role in history. The
spring disappeared under a stream for a number of years, and was
re-discovered by Gideon Putnam. Understanding the importance
of the medicinal spring waters, Putnam, in 1803, leased the land
surrounding Congress Spring and erected a wooden structure around
it. In that same year, Putnam built the Union Hall Hotel to house
visitors to the spring.   In 1805, Putnam leased additional land
adjacent to Congress Spring (and later purchased it in 1807) and laid
out the plan for the village. Despite these improvements to the land,
Dr. John H. Steel, in 1817, described Congress Spring as located
in "an uncultivated piece of ground at the foot of a beautiful little
cascade."

In 1826, Congress Spring was sold to an enterprising New Yorker,
John Clarke, who had owned the first soda shop in New York City.
Clarke built a bottling plant and marketed Saratoga Springs' mineral
water to the world. With profits from his lucrative business, Clarke
acquired additional acres around Congress Spring and created
Congress Park as a place for visitors to Saratoga Springs to promenade
after they sampled the mineral waters to be found in the park. Early
on, a visitor to the park remarked that a "beautiful crescent lawn
… and the classic Doric structure as it originally stood in its simple
beauty over the Congress Spring and the pretty Grecian dome over
the Columbian Spring, are but incidental specimens of the many
improvements" which Clarke made to the property.

In addition to improvements to the park, Clarke fostered the
development of the neighboring houses on Circular Street to the east
of the park. A row of seven stately mansions, not the least of which is

Congress Park Carousel

Clarke's own home, overlooks the park.

Jacob Weidenmann, who worked for the firm of renowned landscape architect Frederick Law Olmsted, was hired to redesign the park in 1875. Congress Park reopened to the public in 1876, just in time for the national centennial celebrations. The curving walking paths had been improved, and a music pavilion, a deer lodge and cafe were built for all to enjoy. The reopening of the park was heralded in all the local papers. From the *Daily Saratogian*, "Congress Park has undergone a transformation which will make the eyes of old visitors stick out with wonder and satisfaction … Indeed the entire place has been putting on 'its best bib and tucker' on account of our One Hundreth birthday…." And, as Stoddard's 1884 guide to Saratoga Springs put it, "No park of similar dimensions in this country excels it in natural beauty, or in elegance of architectural adornments."

Congress Park was privately owned until the city purchased it in stages from 1901 to 1913. In 1877, *The Saratoga Sentinel* reported that 15 1-day admission tickets could be purchased for $1.50 and that two tickets would provide entrance to the park for the evening entertainment.

Today, visitors strolling through Congress Park and the surrounding neighborhood may view the city's architectural and landscape gems, and enjoy sculpture, fountains and works of art by the Victorian Era's leading architects and artists.

❶ ITALIAN GARDENS
Spit and Spat Fountain
1902
Charles Sumner Luce, architect
The Italian Gardens were designed to provide relief from the hot summer sun. The Tritons, "Spit and Spat," are said to represent the Son of Poseidon. They are blowing into conch shells, playfully crouched forward in the water. The streams of water meet in the center of the pool and shatter into a shower. The sculptor of the Spit and Spat fountain is unknown. This beautiful and amusing fountain was carved from Carrara marble and is said to have been added to the

park by Richard Canfield, who wished to bring elegance to the Italian gardens surrounding the Casino through the addition of works of art. The gardens also include a sundial and two Corinthian columns; originally, there were also statues of Hermes and nymphs in the gardens.

② CAROUSEL

1910 Marcus Illions Carousel
2002 Pavilion
John Muse, architect

This beautiful carousel, featuring 28 hand-carved horses, is one of only six existing "Coney Island" style carousels. Sculpted by Marcus Illions, the carousel is the only two-row Illions carousel in existence. It was first used in amusement parks in Ballston Lake and Round Lake and, in 1942, found its "permanent" home at Kaydeross Park, an amusement park on Saratoga Lake. When the amusement park closed in 1987, the carousel was to be auctioned off in pieces. The city of Saratoga Springs purchased the entire carousel, using money contributed by local residents, and painstakingly restored the 28 horses, each of which has a real horsehair tail. Enclosing the carousel is a pavilion, designed by Saratoga Springs architect John Muse. The rounded roof echoes the dome of the Columbian Spring pavilion built by John Clarke.

③ "THE SPIRIT OF LIFE" STATUE

1913 Bronze
Daniel Chester French, sculptor
Henry Bacon, architect

In January 1909, the citizens of Saratoga Springs enthusiastically endorsed a bill to protect the natural resources of the city's springs. The proposal, known as the Reservation Bill, had been developed in response to the depletion of the springs through repeated pumping to extract carbonic gas. Spencer Trask, a great civic leader of Saratoga Springs and prominent New York City financier, was one of the

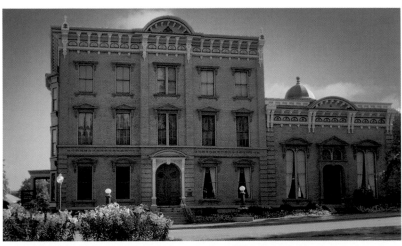

Canfield Casino

I Spirit of Life Statue

leading voices in support of the Reservation bill, and Senator Edgar Truman Brackett, another prominent Saratogian, introduced the bill into the senate. On May 29, 1909, the Reservation Bill creating a New York State Reservation at Saratoga Springs — now known as the Saratoga Spa State Park — was signed by Governor Charles Evans Hughes. Mr. Trask was the Governor's first appointee on the newly created Reservation commission. In December 1909, Spencer Trask was killed in a railroad accident while traveling to New York City on business for the New York State Reservation.

A group of Saratoga Springs citizens commissioned his close friend, Daniel Chester French, sculptor of the statue of Abraham Lincoln for the Lincoln Memorial in Washington D.C., to create a memorial to Trask's life. The artist used his daughter as the model for his winged figure. The statue contains other personal touches evocative of Trask's life. In one hand, the figure holds a bowl overflowing with Saratoga Springs's healing waters, and in the other, clasps an evergreen branch reflecting Trask's love of nature. Trask's personal motto, "For a man's life consisteth not in the abundance of the things which he possesseth." is engraved along the base of the statue.

④ CANFIELD CASINO
1870-1871 Italianate
The Canfield Casino is one of Saratoga Springs' architectural and cultural gems. John Morrissey, a former heavyweight boxing champion and New York State senator, was one of the founders of Saratoga Springs' thoroughbred racing association and, as an offshoot of the track, he opened a gaming club in hopes of attracting August visitors to nighttime gambling. Morrisey's hunch was correct and his Club House became quite successful. Over the years, the club moved to various locations, until 1870, when he built a grand structure in

{ Carlotta Myers }

Summers in Saratoga Springs brought varied entertainments to be enjoyed by visitors and residents alike. For nine years in the 1880's, people gathered afternoons in Congress Park to watch Carlotta Myers, a balloonist, ascend. As the wind lifted the balloon above the trees, Carlotta could be seen waving her handkerchief to the crowds below. Ten minutes later, she would land at Schyuler Junction and board a train on the Boston Hoosac Tunnel and Western line for the four-mile trip back to Saratoga Springs. Carlotta invented the dirigible balloon and was awarded a patent, the first of its kind ever granted to a woman, for its design. Her business partner and husband, Carl, was an aeronautical engineer was in charge of manufacturing the balloons at the Balloon Farm in Frankfort, New York.

Spit

Canfield Casino Window Detail

the center of Congress Park.

Constructed in 1870, the three-story main building is fashioned along the lines of an Italian palazzo. The one-story wing on the east end of the building was added in1871, but before the building was put to use. The building is a powerful expression of the assertive man who conceived of it. Bold detailing, such as the dramatic cornice with four major brackets each drawing a vertical line to the ground and the heavy belt course dividing the first and second stories, is set off by the elegant styling of the varying window pediments. The first floor contained salons, a bar and a large gaming room. Upstairs were private gaming rooms and living quarters.

Following Morrisey's death, the Club House was purchased, in 1894, by the "Prince of Gamblers," Richard Canfield. Canfield was the owner of other successful, upscale casinos in Newport and New York City, and enjoyed hobnobbing with America's social elite. Canfield renamed his gaming parlor The Casino and invested great amounts of money in making improvements. Stained-glass, including some designed and crafted by Louis Comfort Tiffany, was added in the 1890s. In 1903, an addition housing a dining room, kitchen and pantry, was made to the building. Clarence Luce, an architect from New York City, designed the new dining room. The arched coffered ceiling is laid out in a honeycomb pattern and decorated with stained glass windows depicting the 12 zodiac signs. Gaslights hidden in coves in the ceiling created one of the first ever displays of indirect lighting. Air conditioning was virtually unheard of in those days, except in Canfield's Casino. A large fan in the basement forced cool air through pilaster vents in the dining room.

The Casino was a fashionable establishment, offering only the finest food, wine and décor and it attracted the "who's who" of Victorian society, including Cornelius Vanderbilt, William Collins Whitney, J. Pierpont Morgan, actress Lillian Russell and her friend, Diamond Jim Brady. Ladies were only allowed in the dining room. Guests could gamble, dance and dine on innovative gourmet dishes. It is said that the Club Sandwich was invented here under Canfield's ownership.

In 1908, at the height of the gambling reform movement, Richard

Columbian Spring   Spat

Canfield put the Casino up for sale. The village acquired the building in 1911 and combined it with Congress Park, which the Village had also acquired. Over the years, The Casino has had a variety of uses.

By 1922, seeping water had resulted in significant deterioration to the foundation of The Casino's magnificent dining room and the City Council was considering demolition. The Women's Civic League, along with the Saratoga chapter of Daughters of the American Revolution, argued successfully that the same money that the city would spend to demolish the dining room could be spent to restore it. In 1925, Mrs. Adelbert C. Hayden, president of the League, was quoted in *The Saratogian* as saying, "The saving of the Casino demonstrated that concerted action by the women of the community

{Katrina Trask}

Katrina Trask was a writer and philanthropist whose lasting legacy is Yaddo, a retreat center for artists in Saratoga Springs. Born Kate Nichols in 1853, she was raised in Brooklyn and privately educated. Kate married Spencer Trask, an investment banker, in 1874. Kate and Spencer had four children, all of whom died from illnesses in childhood. Their deaths left her despondent and frequently ill. From her childhood on, Kate had an interest in writing and literature but it was not until the late 1880s that she began to write in earnest. Among her earliest works, a set of love poems titled *Under King Constantine*, was published anonymously in 1892. In its second of four printings, the book was published under the name Katrina Trask.

Over the next two decades, Katrina published several more books of poetry. Katrina and Spencer Trask were active in many philanthropies in Saratoga Springs but her greatest work was the development of Yaddo. Believing the estate to be a source of creative inspiration, Katrina began planning for the creation of an artists' colony in 1899. During this period of time, major figures in the world of publishing, business and government visited Yaddo. Spencer Trask died in 1909 in a tragic railroad accident. Eleven years later, Katrina married Spencer's long-time business partner, George Foster Peabody, and they lived at Yaddo until her death in 1922. In June 1926, Yaddo opened its doors for the first time to artists.

Trask Memorial Staircase   View From Trask Memorial Staircase

makes it possible to accomplish the seemingly impossible."

In 1968, The Casino and surrounding land in Congress Park
were threatened by the development of a hotel. A developer had
approached the City Council about building a hotel in the park.
Eager to stimulate economic activity in Saratoga Springs, the City
Council planned to hold a public auction to lease over four acres of
Congress Park for a 150-room hotel. Members of the community
were outraged at the idea of a new hotel in the park. The leader of
a grassroots group opposed to this development brought it to the
attention of Ada Louise Huxtable, architecture critic at *The New York
Times*. One month later, an article in *The Times* brought national
attention to this preservation battle. By mobilizing public and
private pressure against the proposal, the Committee for the Casino
was able to stop the project. And, in 1970, the city was awarded a
federal grant of $116,500 for the rehabilitation of the Casino.

The building was completely restored in 1990 at a cost of $1.1
million and today the dining room and parlor areas continue to
be desirable locations for private functions. The Saratoga History
Museum, which is located in the Casino, houses collections and
exhibits of artifacts from throughout Saratoga Springs' history.

⑤ CONGRESS SPRING PAVILION
Greek Revival
John Clarke marked the site of the Congress Spring for his customers
by erecting a structure resembling a Greek temple. The pavilion you
see today over the Congress Spring is a replica of the original built by
Clarke in the 1830s. Its design is unusual in that there are only three
columns on the narrow end of the pavilion; a typical Greek temple
would have an even number of columns. Unfortunately, repeated
pumping to extract the carbonic gas for use in soda water made the
spring inactive. Today the pavilion shelters one of the park's drinking
fountains, using water piped from nearby Congress I-X Spring to be a
reminder of the park's history.

⑥ COLUMBIAN SPRING PAVILION
Greek Revival
In the 1830s, John Clarke erected a circular temple with a domed

20 Circular St.

roof to house the Columbian Spring; in 1876 this structure and the Congress Spring pavilion were replaced. The present pavilion is comparable in design to the original, although on a smaller, lighter scale. The fountain is now piped with city water.

⑦ KATRINA TRASK MEMORIAL STAIRCASE
1922
Ludlow and Peabody, Architects
Katrina Trask was beloved by the citizens of Saratoga Springs. After her death in 1922, members of Katrina Trask's household commissioned prominent New York City architects Ludlow and Peabody to design a memorial to the "Lady of Yaddo." The staircase, which replaced a flight of worn wooden steps, was constructed of pink Adirondack granite, Mrs. Trask's favorite color.

The steps ascend in an octagonal gothic style with a broad, easy ramp. The gateposts, which are of cast stone, are also designed in the gothic style. An account of the staircase when it was dedicated speaks of the gothic gateposts as signifying the ascent to higher spiritual qualities. Scotland native Robert R. Ritchie, the founder of Petrified Sea Gardens, an historic site of prehistoric fossils in Saratoga Springs, was a stone mason and for a time served on the Saratoga Springs City Council. He and his brother, John, along with Antonio Smaldone, were the stone masons who built the Katrina Trask staircase. Three fossils from the Petrified Sea Gardens can be found on the landings of the staircase.

When it was dedicated in November 1922, hundreds of Saratogians turned out to honor a woman whose philanthropy and hospitality were unparalleled. The staircase is also known as "The Katrina Trask Gateway" and adds beauty to the park while serving to connect pedestrians from the hotels on South Broadway with the park.

⑧ 20 CIRCULAR ST.
Batcheller Mansion
1873 High Victorian Gothic
Charles C. Nichols and John B. Halcott, architects
Built for George Sherman Batcheller, a Civil War officer, New York State assemblyman, and, later, Ambassador to Egypt, this spectacular

38 Circular St.

Veteran's Memorial

house is one of the great treasures of Saratoga Springs' architecture. Batcheller reportedly named the house "Kasr-el-Nouzia," which translates to "Palace of Pleasure." The house, which was designed by the Albany-based firm of Nichols and Halcott, incorporates elements from the German Gothic style, the French Renaissance, the Italianate and others. The tall conical tower is reminiscent of a minaret. Yet the design of the house, while complex, is unified, principally through the horizontal belt that divides the stories and the bay windows that bring the design from the lower stories up through to the roof. Following Batcheller's death in 1908, the house was sold and it passed through a variety of owners. Practically on the brink of demolition in 1973, the house was sold to an owner who restored this exuberant expression of Victorian style. Today, the Batcheller Mansion houses a bed-and-breakfast establishment.

⑨ 24 CIRCULAR ST.

Nolan House
1871-1872 Second Empire
Attributed to Frelin Vaughan, architect
Frelin Vaughan, of the firm of Stevens and Vaughan, is the likely designer of the dramatic house at 24 Circular St.. Mary W. Putnam, widow of Gideon Putnam's grandson, George R. Putnam, purchased it in 1874. The Nolan House stands on a three-acre, heavily treed site. The house is richly ornamented with wrought iron cresting along the roof, vertical polygonal bays with raised towers and a heavily massed porch.

By 1884, Michael N. Nolan and his wife, Anne, owned the house. Nolan was the first Irish mayor of Albany, owner of Beverwyck Brewery, Inc. in Albany, was a steward of the Saratoga Racing Association and raised thoroughbreds in stables located nearby the Nolan estate. The lives of the Nolan and Putnam families were intertwined; it was Blanche Nolan, daughter of Mr. and Mrs. George R. Putnam's son, Francis, who, in 1959, donated the house to St. Peter's Church to be used as a convent by the Sisters of St. Joseph. The Presbyterian-New England Congregational Church purchased the house in 1976.

46 Circular St.   42 Circular St.

⑩ 30 CIRCULAR ST.

Foley House

c. 1885 Queen Anne

The house at 30 Circular St. was most likely built for Augustus Bockes, Saratoga County's first Supreme Court judge, who moved to Circular Street from 1 Franklin Square. A late Victorian Queen Anne style residence, the house shows some influences of the Colonial Revival style in its newer porches. The Foley family owned the house for many years beginning in 1915 until 1948, when it was sold to Skidmore College. The building has a massive vertical feeling, an effect created in part by the tall, narrow, small-paned windows.

⑪ 34 CIRCULAR ST.

Thomas House

c. 1870 Italianate Villa

Dr. Hatfield H. Halstead was most likely the first owner of this residence, which was built about 1870 on land owned originally by John Clarke. The eponymous Thomas House was owned by Henry Thomas, a dentist, from 1893 until his death in 1930; Dr. Thomas left the house to Skidmore College in his will. A design similar to this house appears in Samuel Sloan's *Homestead Architecture* (1861). The house has all of the classic features of an Italianate Villa. The L-shaped plan with a tower nestled into the angle is characteristic of the style. The tower on this house, as on many of the other significant residences in Saratoga Springs, provided a space from which residents of the house could view the glories of nature. For the owners of 34 Circular St., its magnificent views of Congress Park and of summer sunsets must indeed provide a sublime vista.

⑫ 38 CIRCULAR ST.

Harsha House

1870 Italianate Villa

David A. Harsha, a broker, built 38 Circular St. after acquiring the lot from Eliza Sheehan, John Clarke's daughter, in 1870. This villa has been called a masterpiece of Italianate design. It is completely symmetrical. Among the notable details of the house, are the protruding central bay with a palladian-like window, below the pediment, a multi-faceted cornice and the centrally placed observatory or belvedere. It was turned into apartments in 1941 and

1 Spit and Spat Italian Gardens

eventually it was sold to Skidmore College, which named it "Harsha House." In 1977, the house was restored to private ownership.

⑬ 42 CIRCULAR ST.

1874 Italianate Villa

Originally built in 1874 for Augustine W. Shepherd, an attorney with the law firm of Shepherd and Tefft, this building was the home of a Dominican convent from 1942 to 1959 when it was purchased by Skidmore College. The house was sold to private owners in 1964. This unusual High Victorian Italianate Villa marries the tall tower of the country villa with the standard Italianate city house. The large tower rises three stories up. The arched windows underneath the eaves are separated from the second story below by horizontal banding. Also of note are the multi-paned windows on the first floor.

⑭ 46 CIRCULAR ST.

Clarke House

1832 Greek Revival

This beautifully preserved Greek Revival house was built for John Clarke, the man who made the waters of Saratoga Springs world famous. It is believed that Clarke hired John Hodgman, builder of both 129 and 127 Circular St., to design his house. Though architecturally earlier than the other buildings in the area, the house, with its massive square pillars, temple front and steps, complements the neighborhood. The house was purchased in 1941 by Skidmore College for use as the home of the president of college. In 1975, Skidmore relocated its president's house to 760 North Broadway. Today the house is privately owned.

Sources:
The Gazette, June 3, 2001
Coward, Jr., Wheaton. A Guide to Saratoga, Coronet Press, Inc., Saratoga Springs, N.Y. 1990.
Merrill, Arthur A. Confessions of Congress Park Saratoga Springs-New York, Arthur A. Merrill, Saratoga Springs, N.Y. 1955.
Stoddard's Saratoga Springs. R. Stoddard, Glens Falls, N.Y., 1884.
Waite, Marjorie Peabody. Seeing Saratoga, a Scenic and Historic Guide in Twenty-Two Trips, 1935.
Kettlewell, James K. Saratoga Springs An Architectural History, Lyrical Ballad Book Store, Saratoga Springs, 1991.
The Nineteenth-century Architecture of Saratoga Springs, Architecture Worth Saving in New York State, New York State Council on the Arts, 1970.
O'Connor, Eugene. The Casino, Historical Society of Saratoga Springs, 1987 edition.

UNION AVENUE

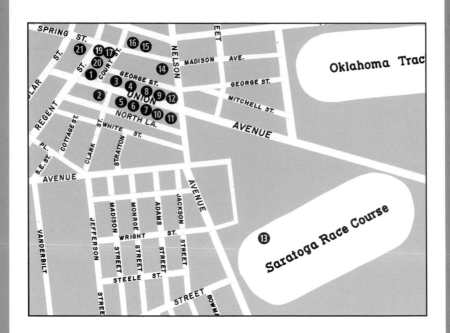

TOUR DETAILS

Distance: 0.9 miles

Steps: 1,889

Time: Approximately 25 minutes

Terrain: Flat

Directions: Start at Circular St. and Union Ave. East on Union Ave. to Nelson Ave., north on Nelson Ave. to Spring St., west on Spring St. to Regent St., south on Regent St. to Union Ave.

TOUR HIGHLIGHTS

❶ 31 Union Ave.

❷ 48 Union Ave.

❸ 73 Union Ave.

❹ 85 Union Ave.

❺ 88 Union Ave.

❻ 100 Union Ave.

❼ 104 Union Ave.

❽ 107 Union Ave.

❾ 115 Union Ave.

❿ 120 Union Ave.

⓫ 124 Union Ave.

⓬ 125 Union Ave.

⓭ Saratoga Race Course

⓮ 176 Spring St.

⓯ 149 Spring St.

⓰ 147 Spring St.

⓱ 112 Spring St.

⓲ 110 Spring St. (not on map)

⓳ 108 Spring St.

⓴ 148 Regent St.

㉑ 153 Regent St.

$\mathcal{T}$oday Union Avenue is a majestic, tree-lined, four-lane road, but 175 years ago it was a narrow dirt path. A rough, bumpy road, it still met the needs of Saratogians and visitors for basic travel between two major attractions – Congress Spring and Saratoga Lake. This well-traveled path became an official road in the 1840s, named East Congress Street. It was a continuation of Congress Street through the park and across Circular Street.

During the Civil War, the road was renamed Union Avenue, a reflection, perhaps, of the pride Saratogians took in the Union Army. Toward the close of the war, in 1863, thoroughbred horse racing came to Saratoga Springs at a track "out Union Avenue," and Union Avenue became the place to be seen. During the days and eventually the weeks of the race meet, carriages lined the avenue waiting to drop off their fashionable passengers at the track.

The residential neighborhoods in the city were expanding east along Spring Street and along Regent Street and by the late 1860s, similar signs of growth could be found in the new houses being built along Union Avenue. The neighborhood developed over the remaining decades of the 19th century. Some houses were built by year-round residents who rented their homes out during the summer, and others were used only during the season. While quite magnificent in their own right, most of the houses and summer cottages on Union Avenue were modest in comparison to the majestic residences on North Broadway.

In 1911, the city acquired the Canfield Casino and sections of Congress Park. It closed off Union Avenue at Circular Street to create the park as it is today. Union Avenue provides one of the main entrances to the city, and visitors who travel into the city on Union Avenue during the summer are treated to the vibrant flowerbeds that mark a pedestrian entrance to Congress Park.

As the popularity of gambling and horse racing faded in Saratoga Springs, many of the grand residences on Union Avenue and the

Union Avenue

surrounding streets were abandoned by their owners and a number of these buildings were purchased by Skidmore College. The college occupied much of the Union Avenue area of town from the early 1900s until the mid-1960s. Some of these Queen Anne style buildings with their generous porches and fabulous turrets became home to "Skiddies" and to members of the college's faculty. Other buildings were put to use as classrooms and offices. When Skidmore moved its campus to North Broadway in 1966, its holdings in the Union Avenue area were sold. Today, many of these same buildings are apartments and condominiums.

❶ 31 UNION AVE.
c. 1873 High Victorian, c. 1920 Colonial Revival Remodel
This residence is one of the first constructed on Union Avenue. Originally built in the High Victorian style, the house went through an extensive renovation in the 1920s and emerged as an example of Colonial Revival architecture. During this renovation, the porch, dormers and bay windows were added.

❷ 48 UNION AVE.
Salisbury House
c. 1905 Colonial Revival
This house, with its majestic curved portico and great sweeping porches on both the first and second stories, was built by Wilson W. Butler, a New York City steel manufacturer, as a summer cottage. The house boasted a billiard room, gymnasium and extensive stable. Mr. Butler sold the house in 1925 to a court stenographer, Josiah G. Salisbury. Mr. Salisbury was forced to sell the house in 1936 to Skidmore College as he had gone bankrupt. The college named the house Salisbury House. It was later converted to offices.

❸ 73 UNION AVE.
1883 High Victorian Gothic
Attributed to Frelin Vaughan
This house was built for John M. Jones, about whom no information survives. Between 1932 and 1934, this house was the home of Saratoga Springs architect William Vaughan. Notable features on the

house include lathe-turned balusters on the great open porch, and the vertical line of a tower built into the façade that continues from the entrance through the top of the high-peaked roof. Two horizontal bands, one under the eaves textured with fish-scale shingles and one below the second story windows detailed with stars, help unify this beautifully complex example of High Victorian Gothic architecture.

❹ 85 UNION AVE.
1874 Italianate
Ashabel Moody, a carpenter, was the first owner of this house. For several years in the 1890s, it was the home of Benjamin Judson, publisher of *The Saratogian*, and his wife, Elizabeth. Where most of the houses on Union Avenue have porches facing it, the Colonial Revival porches on this residence, which were added later, are on the east and west sides of the building. An interesting element of the façade is the bracketed cornices above the windows. The front door has 12-paned sidelight windows. On the second floor of the house is a small chapel.

❺ 88 UNION AVE.
c.1868 High Victorian Gothic
This residence was likely built for George U. and Eliza Gates. Gates began his career as a tinsmith. Together with his son, Odell, Gates founded Gates & Co. Hardware that was located at 460 Broadway for many years. The angularity and massing of this house reveal a blend of the High Victorian Gothic and Queen Anne styles of architecture. The paired porch posts suggest the Colonial Revival style, an indication perhaps, that the unusual five-sided pavilion porch was built or rebuilt later.

❻ 100 UNION AVE.
c. 1850 Greek Revival
Believed to be the oldest house on Union Avenue, this lovely cottage had a variety of owners and tenants from its construction

73 Union Ave.

1 110 Spring St.

date to about 1884, when it was purchased by Robert C. Fonda, a businessman who owned a boot and shoe store on Broadway. In 1942, it became the Dean's House for Skidmore College. Since 1977, the cottage has been a private residence. It is a simple Victorian dwelling, probably built by a carpenter. The structure is stucco without the normal half-timbering effect. The roofs are peaked and a turned balustrade decorates the front porch.

⑦ 104 UNION AVE.
c. 1874 High Victorian Gothic

A grocer and flour and grain dealer, Deyoe Lohnas and his wife, Huldah, built this house around 1874. The original style was High Victorian Gothic. A Queen Anne porch was added later. The design is vertically oriented with the arrangement of rooflines and arched window lintels drawing the eye upward to the fish-scale shingles decorating the roof gable. A horizontal belt of evenly spaced brackets running along the first story porch eaves balances the strong verticality. Hervey Leonard bought the house in 1887, and then subsequently rented it to a variety of well-to-do summer tenants from New York, Albany and New Orleans. During this time, the house was significantly remodeled and the Colonial Revival porches and pavilions on the first and second stories were added. From 1935 to 1937, Dr. Wallace F. MacNaughton operated his MacNaughton Sanitarium here. In 1946, Skidmore College acquired the property, named it Kimball House, and used it as a dormitory. Today this house, with its beautiful porches, is a private residence.

⑧ 107 UNION AVE.
Grande House
c. 1885 High Victorian Gothic
S. Gifford Slocum, architect

Designed by architect S. Gifford Slocum, this house was built in about 1885 for Dr. Burney J. Kendall. The unusual candle snuffer cap at one end of the porch, balanced by a tower at the opposite corner of the façade, have the visual effect of giving the house a strong vertical thrust. The High Victorian Gothic porch wraps around the building and lends a certain solidity to the building. Of note is the decorative flowers banded around the top of the porch and below the third story. This floral motif is reflected also in panels on the upper story of the tower and in the applied decoration in the gable.

⑨ 115 UNION AVE.
Ross House
c. 1885 Queen Anne
Attributed to S. Gifford Slocum, architect

Frank White, a partner in Ingham, White and Co. (insurance) was

Saratoga Race Course

the original owner of this residence that is thought to have been designed by S. Gifford Slocum. Rock-faced masonry lies solidly on the ground and changes in the stories above to shingles, then to stucco and half-timber work. This use of materials may reflect the influence of architect Stanford White, and is similar to Slocum's designs for the Annandale Mansion and the Lawton Villa on Clinton Street. The design of the building uses breadth rather than ornament to convey a feeling of solidity. This effect is reinforced by the heavy Richardsonian arched doorway. In 1952, Skidmore College purchased the house. The college sold it when it moved to its new campus on North Broadway.

⑩ 120 UNION AVE.
Ketchum House
c. 1890 Queen Anne
The major architectural style of Union Avenue can be found in this and neighboring structures. The Ketchum House has a rock-faced masonry foundation and shingle-covered upper stories. Stone quoins accentuate the angles of the first story and are carried through the second story of the tower. These angles are softened on the second-story balcony. Slender porch columns rise on the porch and a polygonal tower crowns the building. The house, which was once a private residence, has been altered to accommodate apartments.

⑪ 124 UNION AVE.
c. 1885 High Victorian Gothic
The style of this house is transitional – principally High Victorian Gothic – yet some of the important architectural elements are firmly rooted in the Queen Anne style. The relatively compact façade belies the heavy massing of the building. Of note is the texturing of this house in the stucco, half timbering and shingles and how that contributes to the heavy mass of the house. The Queen Anne porch rises gracefully in the corner of the polygonal tower. Upper-story

balconies and porches add further lightness to this substantial house. Unlike its neighbors, this house has always been a private residence.

⑫ 125 UNION AVE.
Van Deusen House
c. 1905 Colonial Revival

This house was originally was built as a summer residence for Mirabeau L. Towne of Brooklyn, in a variation on the Colonial Revival style, which is unusual for the Union Avenue neighborhood. The house features a steep roof with dormers, which has its origins in the Georgian Colonial. The colonnaded porch, with its square columns supporting a bold pediment, is Greek Revival. The glass around the doorway reflects the influence of the Federal style. Sam Riddle, owner of famed racehorse Man O' War and prominent player at the Saratoga Race Course, summered here from 1918 through 1950. In 1951, Skidmore College bought the house and named it East House. The college changed the name of the building in 1963 to the Van Deusen House, perhaps in honor of Charles C. Van Deusen, who had been president of the Adirondack Trust Company in the 1920s and 1930s. Like many of the grand homes along Union Avenue, the building was sold when the college moved its campus to North Broadway.

⑬ SARATOGA RACE COURSE
1902

A notorious gambler, John Morrissey opened the inaugural race meet on the race track in Saratoga Springs on Aug. 3,1863. The original track was located on the north side of Union Avenue across from the present race course. The first race meet offered four days of racing, with two races each day. Morrisey's venture was so successful that by the next year it had outgrown its original track. The Saratoga Racing Association built a new facility on the south side of Union Avenue, the site of the present Saratoga Race Course.

The first grandstand built for the new track was a large structure, but not particularly distinguished in its architecture. In 1902, the Saratoga Racing Association, led by William Collins Whitney, invested in rebuilding the track area. The Saratoga Race Course today comprises more than 200 buildings, including the two race tracks, barns, outbuildings, the Jockey Club and the resident manager's house on Union Avenue. The finest of these is the grandstand, with its soaring turreted roof, built in 1902 under the direction of landscape architect Charles Leavitt of New York City. Despite renovations over the years, the track buildings retain their Victorian splendor and remain an important site in the history of American horse racing.

1 Saratoga Race Course

147 Spring St.

149 Spring St.

⑭ 176 SPRING ST.

1869 Italianate with High Victorian Gothic Gable

In 1869, John H. White of Schenectady leased a lot, house and a soda-water manufacturing business at this location to Robert Weller, and his wife, Eliza, for a period of two years. According to their contract with White, at the end of two years the Wellers could purchase the property and business for $5,000, which they did. Robert Weller went on to make a name for himself in the soda water business. Of note is the screen detailing in the gable with the rounded arch presenting a contrast to the sharp peak of the roof and echoing the double-arched window with a diamond-shaped hood on the third story.

⑮ 149 SPRING ST.

c. 1863 Vernacular

Stephen Trumbell is believed to have built this house on land he purchased in 1862 from John H. White, who also owned the property at 176 Spring St. It is not clear what Mr. Trumbull's occupation was, however, he is thought to have been employed by Dr. John Perry at the Adelphi Hotel. Eliza A. Ensign ran a boarding house here from 1884 to 1890. It is a modest cottage nestled in a

{ Anne Clare }

The longest tenure of any superintendent of the Saratoga Race Course was that of Anne Clare, who held the position from 1940 to 1960. At that time, Anne Clare was the only woman race course superintendent in the nation. She came to the position when her husband died suddenly in 1940. Tom Clare had been superintendent for 16 years. A 1946 article in *The Racing Digest* noted that Anne "worked sided by side with her husband, learning every nook and cranny of the vast plant under his jurisdiction, to say nothing of every detail connected with its operation." Soon after taking the reins of the race course, Anne oversaw the conversion of bookmaking stalls to the newly legalized pari-mutuel windows. She was known for her attention to detail and for her ability to take on all problems. Anne was also a noted horticulturist and began the program of plantings at the race course that continues today, making it a horticultural showplace. She died in 1976, at the age of 84.

Regent Street

neighborhood marked by extroverted Queen Anne style houses, but the tall narrow windows on the first story and the two-story bay on the right side of the house add interest to the otherwise simple design.

⑯ 147 SPRING ST.

c. 1867 Queen Anne

This house was the residence of William Gibbs, a merchant in the flour and grain business. The house features a variety of textures in the building — the façade is ornate, with a three-story projecting bay, and on the first and second stories are enclosed bay windows, but on the third story the bay opens up as a porch. The elaborate hipped roof emphasizes the vertical orientation of the design.

⑰ 112 SPRING ST.

School No. 4

c. 1911 Beaux-Arts

This is the third school building to be built on this site. The first two were so poorly constructed, they were considered unsafe for children and were demolished. From its opening in 1911 through about 1978, children were welcomed into this solidly built brick building through the classically styled entrance marked by one-and-a-half story stone columns. For a period of time, School No. 4 was the only public school in Saratoga Springs with a cafeteria that provided hot lunches for its students. No longer used as a school, the building retains its original interior detail and classrooms are now used as offices. While largely without ornamentation, the building conveys a sense of orderliness and presence through the regularity and symmetry of the window pattern, its strong entrance and the row of large dentils below the overhanging eaves.

⑱ 110 SPRING ST.

1870 Lombardian Romanesque

The latter half of the 19th century saw Saratoga Springs growing at a phenomenal rate. Its churches were keeping pace with the needs of the community. During this time several missions and chapels were formed in the village. This Romanesque style church building with corbelled brickwork and stone was completed in 1870 for Newland Mission Chapel. In August 1871, the Second Presbyterian Church formed and located in the chapel. As the Presbyterian Church grew,

112 Spring St.   148 Regent St.

its membership decided to build a new church, and sold the building to the Second Baptist Church, which worshiped there until 1917. The Saratoga Gospel Tabernacle began holding services in the church in 1919. The building now houses an art gallery and the offices of several non-profit organizations.

⑲ 108 SPRING ST.
c. 1900 Four Square
This house was first a residence for the Rev. Herbert M. Gesner, pastor of the Second Presbyterian Church. This simple house has a hipped roof with a dormer window typical of the Four Square style. The house may have been renovated in the 1920s, as the details, particularly the windows, reflect the Craftsman style that was introduced in that era. The residence was purchased by Skidmore College and used as classrooms and offices. It is now a private home.

⑳ 148 REGENT ST.
1863 Italianate
This classic Italianate building with its flat roof, heavy brackets and cupola is unique in the city because of its unusual porches, particularly the open porch on the second floor and the graceful latticework on the first-floor porch.

㉑ 153 REGENT ST.
Regent Street Theater
1903 Colonial Revival
William Vaughan, architect
This 15,400-square-foot building was constructed in 1903 as the Young Women's Industrial Club, precursor to Skidmore College. Its interior featured large spacious rooms, fireplaces and skylights. In the 1930s, the first floor of the building was converted to a theater and gymnasium. In 1977, Skidmore College sold the building, but by 1980, it was in need of significant repair and in bank receivership. To save the building from demolition, the bank that owned it donated it to the Saratoga Springs Preservation Foundation. Using grant money, the Preservation Foundation stabilized the building and sold it at auction to W.J. Grande & Son. The company restored the building and converted it to an antique center.

Around the

TRACK

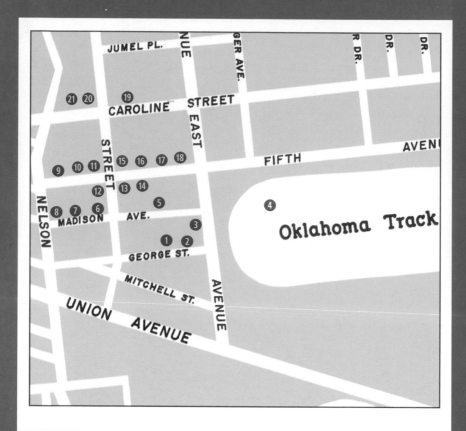

TOUR DETAILS

Distance: 1.6 miles

Steps: 3,378

Time: Approximately 40 minutes

Terrain: Flat, with some uneven sidewalks

Directions: Start on George St., just west of East Ave.. George St. east to East Ave. North on East Ave. to Madison Ave.. West on Madison Ave. to Nelson Ave.. North on Nelson Ave. to Fifth Ave.. East on Fifth Ave. to East Ave.. North on East Ave. to Caroline St.. West on Caroline St. to Nelson Ave.. South on Nelson Ave. to George St.. East on George St. to beginning.

TOUR HIGHLIGHTS

❶ 95 George St.

❷ 111 George St.

❸ 250 East Ave.

❹ Oklahoma Track

❺ 33 Madison Ave.

❻ 21 Madison Ave.

❼ 5 Madison Ave.

❽ 1 Madison Ave.

❾ 1 Fifth Ave.

❿ 9 Fifth Ave.

⓫ 15 Fifth Ave.

⓬ 20 Fifth Ave.

⓭ 24 Fifth Ave.

⓮ 28 Fifth Ave.

⓯ 29 Fifth Ave.

⓰ 33 Fifth Ave.

⓱ 37 Fifth Ave.

⓲ 43 Fifth Ave.

⓳ 221-223 Caroline St.

⓴ 205 Caroline St.

㉑ 203 Caroline St.

Much of the neighborhood adjacent to the Saratoga Race Course was once known as "The Wellington Lots." Most of the houses in this area were built during the post-Civil War boom. The land, which had previously belonged to the renowned Saratoga Springs bottling plant owner, John Clarke, was sold in 1869 by Clarke's daughter, Eliza, and her husband, Cornelius Sheehan, the vice president and secretary of the Congress and Empire Spring Company. The purchaser was William Wellington, an enterprising railroad contractor from North Oxford, Massachusetts.

Having seen the popularity of the new thoroughbred race course, which had opened "Out Union Avenue," Wellington surmised he could develop land adjacent to the track and turn a tidy profit. He purchased the property for $22,000 and began planning a subdivision.

The property was divided into 56 building lots but Wellington never saw houses built here, as he died in June of 1872 before any construction started. The Wellington children, Charles, Willis and Charlotte, sold their first building lot a little more than a month after their father's death. After 25 years, only 16 houses had been constructed on the Wellington Lots. The Wellington family continued to sell building lots until 1919, including the site of the Fasig-Tipton Pavilion and stables.

Today, Mr. Wellington's dream has come to fruition. The Wellington Lots neighborhood on the East Side of the city welcomes visitors each summer racing season as vacationers and horsemen converge on Saratoga Springs to experience the excitement of the thoroughbred races. As the neighborhood grew up over several generations, the evolution of architectural taste and style from simple to grand may be seen in the various residences lining the streets.

Humphrey S. Finney Pavillion

119 George St.

❶ 95 GEORGE ST.
c. 1880 Victorian Gothic Stick Style
This house was first home to tinsmith Nelson Bootier. It is a simple house, so typical of vernacular houses found throughout Saratoga Springs, but still shows attention to detail in the design. Of note is the front gable with fish-scale shingles and elaborate carved panels below the porch eaves.

❷ 111 GEORGE ST.
c. 1883 Victorian Vernacular
James Arnold, a carpenter, and Edward Arnold, a driver, were the first owners of the house at 111 George St.. By 1888, another Arnold, Theodore, who was a brass finisher, gold and silver plater, and bronzer, had purchased the residence. Similar to the house at 95 George St., this simple Victorian dwelling reveals attention to detail in design, particularly in the arched window hoods.

❸ 250 EAST AVE.
Fasig-Tipton Stables
Humphrey S. Finney Pavilion
c. 1972 Modern
In 1898, respected horseman Edward A. Tipton joined forces with Civil War veteran William B. Fasig to create the country's premiere thoroughbred sales company. Fasig-Tipton experienced great success until 1910, when during the reform movement, racing was stopped in New York. Fasig-Tipton subsequently moved its horse auction business to Kentucky, a locale that still welcomed horse racing. In 1918, Fasig-Tipton returned to Saratoga Springs and, in that year, the great Man O' War was sold at Saratoga Springs as a yearling. Each August, the thoroughbred yearling sale held in the Humphrey S. Finney Pavilion, named for a former president and chief auctioneer of Fasig-Tipton, continues to be a highlight of Saratoga Springs' racing season. The pavilion is one of the few examples of modern architecture in Saratoga Springs. Its rounded shape reflects the functionality of the building as an auditorium. The materials — glass, concrete and wood – provide the only texture in the stark design.

④ OKLAHOMA TRACK
1904

From as early as 1847, racing has been a part of Saratoga Springs. The first race track was a simple dirt track built for the New York State Fair. Several thousand fans were on hand for opening day. Sixteen years later, John Morrissey leased the Saratoga Trotting Course, as it had become known, for the first thoroughbred race meet. The earliest grandstand section was a wooden structure but most spectators chose to view the races from their carriages. Thoroughbred racing became so popular that one year later, in 1864, a new track was built across Union Avenue to the south. By the 1880s, the Saratoga Trotting Course, nicknamed Horse Haven, was used as a training track for thoroughbreds. In 1902, William Collins Whitney, president of the Saratoga Association for the Improvement of the Breed of Horses, purchased 120 acres, including Horse Haven, and built yearling stables, a training track, and housing for track workers. Today, the Oklahoma Track, built in 1904, is the training track and Horse Haven is used as a service road. From a vantage point on East Avenue, visitors can view horses warming up on this track in the early mornings throughout the summer.

⑤ 33 MADISON AVE.
c. 1921 Colonial Revival

This residence was built for Emery Jones, a salesman and superintendent of the adjacent Fasig-Tipton Stables. In 1968, Fasig-Tipton purchased the house for use during race seasons by its directors. Coming full circle, the house is once again a private residence. An interesting detail of this house is the design of the top half of each window.

⑥ 21 MADISON AVE.
c. 1902 Colonial Revival

This house, built at the beginning of the 20th century, has been a single-family residence, was operated as "The Elmwood" with tourist accommodations, and was converted to apartments in the 1940s. Among the architectural details to notice about this house are the

Horse Haven Track

143 Fifth Ave.

brackets underneath the eaves, a large gabled dormer in the center of the house, and a three-sided porch with elegant columns and delicate balusters.

❼ 5 MADISON AVE.

c.1898 Queen Anne
R. Newton Brezee, architect
This residence was originally built for George N. Montanye, a merchant dealing in coal, wood and masons' supplies. The three-story, cross-gabled house has a wide porch wrapping around to the left.

❽ 1 MADISON AVE.

1872 Second Empire
Built in the autumn of 1872 for Benjamin F. Walker, who owned the drugstore Groesbeck & Company at 180 Broadway, this house was the first in the subdivision. The mansard roof is dominated by an Italianate tower which rises above the portico. Notice how the house is set high on a basement, which is lit by rounded windows. The typical Victorian bay windows on the right and left side of the house were added later; the variation in the window shape and decoration is a hint that these were an addition to the original building.

❾ 1 FIFTH AVE

1883 Victorian Gothic Stick Style
S. Gifford Slocum, architect
This residence was designed by S. Gifford Slocum for Robert H. Trim, a plumber and gas fitter, whose family owned the house until about 1960. Typical of Slocum's designs, the house is interesting from all angles. The asymmetrical, three-dimensional design is meant

{ THE TRIM WOMEN }

Margaret Trim and her daughters, Clara and Margaret, were spirited and resourceful entrepreneurs. While their story is not unique in Saratoga Springs, the Trim women exemplify the enterprising women of their time. When her husband and the father of her children abandoned them to pursue his dream of a better life, Mrs. Trim reacted by converting their home into a boarding house enabling her to support her daughters and herself. When Mr. Trim returned to Saratoga Springs some years later, he was not welcomed back into the Trim women's household. Following Mrs. Trim's death in 1919, Clara became mistress of the boarding house. Another daughter, Margaret, had opened the Skidmore Tea Room and Gift Shop at 92 Spring St. in 1914, and later moved it to Broadway. After Clara died, Margaret again relocated the tea room, sometimes called the House of Trim, to the house at 1 Fifth Ave. and operated it there until 1960.

1 Fifth Ave.

to mirror nature, resisting the classic formality of earlier architectural styles. By 1889, Trim had a hardware store at 420 Broadway but seven years later he gave up the business and went to work as a salesman for the G.F. Harvey Company, pharmaceutical manufacturers whose headquarters were on Wells Street in Saratoga Springs. His career at the Harvey Company was short-lived and a year later, Mr. Trim became a traveling salesman for Lincoln Spring Company in Boston. The Trims, like many Saratogians then and now, rented their house during the racing season and took up residence elsewhere in the city. One of the prominent summer residents of the house was George Bull, president of the Saratoga Racing Association in the 1930s.

⑩ 9 FIFTH AVE.
c. 1895 Queen Anne
In 1885 the Wellingtons sold two lots for $3,200 to Martin Lefler, a grocer at 442 Broadway, on one of which this house was eventually built. The second lot passed through three more owners until, in 1895, Anna Augusta Lockwood, whose home at 5 Fifth Ave. was adjacent to the lots, sold the eastern portion and built 9 Fifth Ave. on the remaining land. The three-story, four-bay classic Queen Anne style house is typical of the period.

⑪ 15 FIFTH AVE.
c. 1872 Second Empire
Gilbert Croff, architect
This residence was designed by Gilbert Croff for David F. Ritchie. Ritchie and his partner, Charles F. Paul, were proprietors of the *Daily Saratogian* and *Weekly Saratogian* and were book and job printers. One of the highlights of the house is the four-story tower on the left side of the front facade. The distinctive, steeply pitched mansard-like roof on the tower is similar to those found in many of Croff's published residential designs. Worth noting is the delicate detailing of the decorative wood-trim surround on all of the windows. The full-width, flat-roof porch has trim and brackets only along the façade and has no balustrade.

⑫ 20 FIFTH AVE.

c.1890 Queen Anne/Shingle Style

One of the most notable aspects of this generous house with its asymmetrical and irregular roofline is the round tower and stone chimney built into the left side of the façade. The house also features a variety of window shapes and sizes, and various patterns of leaded windows.

⑬ 24 FIFTH AVE.

1900 Colonial Revival

John N. Huyck of Albany built this house in 1900 on land he purchased from Brooklyn land speculator Eugene F. O'Connor, who bought many of the Wellington Lots between 1886 and 1888. Mr. Huyck was never a year-round resident of Saratoga Springs and he may have used the house as a summer cottage. One of the interesting aspects of this residence is the variety of window shapes and sizes.

⑭ 28 FIFTH AVE.

c. 1900 Colonial Revival

28 Fifth Ave. is a perfect example of the Colonial Revival style from the turn of the 19th century. Among the distinctive features of the house are the broad, shallow bay windows and the porch with Roman Doric columns, Italian Renaissance balusters, and a small gable over the entranceway. The broad, double-hung windows were also typical of the style. Notice particularly the X-like pattern in muntins of the roof windows; this window detail is the one Beaux-Arts feature from France, not America, and is a detail borrowed from ancient Rome.

⑮ 29 FIFTH AVE.

1915 Craftsman

This fine example of a Craftsman bungalow was built for Alfred S. Clark and his wife, Lena. Clark was the secretary of the Clark Textile Company, which was located on High Rock Avenue. The Clarks

29 Fifth Ave.

37 Fifth Ave.

20 Fifth Ave.

lived here until their move to Glens Falls in 1921. The residence, which has had a number of owners over the years, retains classic elements of the Craftsman period, including the cobblestone walls of the first-story porch, and the large central dormer with a balcony.

⑯ 33 FIFTH AVE.
c. 1915 Craftsman

On a street with a number of Craftsman bungalows, the house at 33 Fifth is unique for the two-story porte-cochere on the right side. Notice also the row of three lovely leaded windows in the front dormer.

⑰ 37 FIFTH AVE.
c. 1929 Tudor
William H. Vaughan, architect

This charming Tudor was built for Edgar F. Hewitt, a grocer, and his wife, Grace, who lived here until 1948 when the residence was sold to Frederick K. Tarrant and his wife, Jane. Tarrant was then president of the Tarrant Manufacturing Company, Inc., which specialized in welding and road building equipment. The house is a wonderful example of the Tudor style that was popular between 1890 and 1940. Of particular note is the steeply pitched roof, the decorative half-timbering in the gable ends, tall narrow windows, and on the left side of the house, the chimney crowned by decorative chimney pots.

⑱ 43 FIFTH AVE.
c. 1920 Colonial Revival
William H. Vaughan, architect

Built after 1920, this house was owned in the 1930s by Walter and Ethel Fullerton. Mr. Fullerton was a partner in the law firm of Leary & Fullerton and was a vice-president and trust officer of Saratoga National Bank. Fullerton and his partner, James A. Leary, whose home was at 779 Broadway, hired the same architect to renovate their residences in the 1940s. As a result, the master bath, complete with opulent shower with both overhead and horizontal showerheads, is exactly the same in the two residences. The house at 43 Fifth Ave. has a wealth of elegant detailing. Take note of the impressive porch with fluted Corinthian columns holding up a pediment which has a delicate fanlight, and transom lights surrounding the front door.

221 - 223 Caroline St.

⑲ 221-223 CAROLINE ST.
c. 1870 Italianate Duplex
Constructed around 1870, this residence was purposely built as a
two-family dwelling. Its owners and tenants included a watchmaker
and a slater. The heavy bracket in the center of the cornice creates a
subtle suggestion of the vertical separation between the two units.

⑳ 215 CAROLINE ST.
c. 1886 Queen Anne
David E. Kirkpatrick and his wife, Emma, built this house.
Kirkpatrick and his brothers owned a livery business on Ludlow
Street. Through the years, Kirkpatrick had a variety of jobs and
in 1888 he became the manager of the Hotel Todd, located at
398 Broadway. An advertisement for the Hotel Todd touted it as
"Headquarters for D. G. Yuengling, Jr.'s Lager - Always on Draft."
Eleven years later, when the hotel changed hands, Kirkpatrick went
on the road as a traveling salesman for a liquor company and took
up residence in New York City. Kirkpatrick is said to have enjoyed
the gaming pursuits offered in Saratoga Springs and money was not
plentiful for the family of seven. According to a descendent of the
Kirkpatrick family, the house was built in stages, as Mrs. Kirkpatrick
had to "pinch" money from her husband's winnings to complete
construction. Following her husband's departure, Mrs. Kirkpatrick
converted her house into two apartments, living in one and renting
out the other. The residence remained a duplex until 1984, when
it was purchased and restored to a single-family home. Among the
unusual and elegant details of this house are the six-gabled roof, the
projecting bay window on the left side of the house and the extensive
use of stained glass windows.

㉑ 203 CAROLINE ST.
c. 1870 High Victorian
This residence, similar to its neighbors, features gable detailing at
the front of the house. Take note of the fanlight above the arched
doorway. Behind the house is the original carriage house, now a
garage.

Sources:
Cary, Andrew. "Building the Standard at Saratoga," Saratoga Journal, Thoroughbred
Times. September 2, 2003.

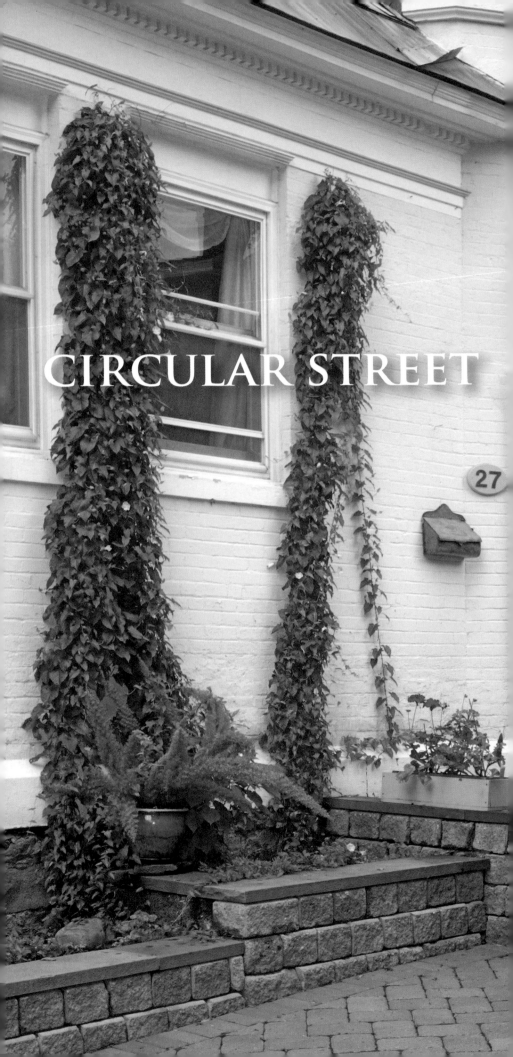

CIRCULAR STREET

27

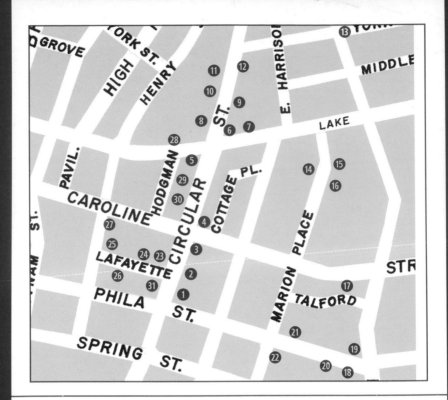

TOUR DETAILS

Distance: 1.75 miles

Steps: 3,500

Time: Approximately 45 minutes

Terrain: Mostly flat, with one small incline. Some uneven sidewalks.

Directions: (Note: The tour follows roughly a figure-8.) Start at Phila and Circular Sts. North on Circular St., cross Lake Ave, to York St. East on York Ave to Harrison St. South on Harrison St. to Lake Ave. East on Lake Ave to Marion Pl. South on Marion Pl. to Talford Pl. East on Talford Pl. to Nelson Ave. South on Nelson Ave. to Phila St. West on Phila St. to Circular St. North on Circular St. to Lafayette St. West on Lafayette St. to Henry St. North on Henry St. to Lake Ave. East on Lake Ave. to Circular St. South on Circular St. to Phila St.

TOUR HIGHLIGHTS

❶ 102 Circular St.

❷ 108 Circular St.

❸ 120 Circular St.

❹ 122 Circular St.

❺ 137 Circular St.

❻ 105 Lake Ave.

❼ 107 Lake Ave.

❽ 155 Circular St.

❾ 162 Circular St.

❿ 163 Circular St.

⓫ 173 Circular St.

⓬ 172 Circular St.

⓭ 43 York Ave.

⓮ 19 Marion Place

⓯ 20 Marion Place

⓰ 26 Marion Place

⓱ 14 Talford Place

⓲ 184 Phila St.

⓳ 181 Phila St.

⓴ 180 Phila St.

㉑ 159 Phila St.

㉒ 150 Phila St.

㉓ 115 Circular St.

㉔ 27 Layfayette St.

㉕ 15 Lafayette St.

㉖ 14 Lafayette St.

㉗ 60 Henry St.

㉘ 61 Lake Ave.

㉙ 129 Circular St.

㉚ 127 Circular St.

㉛ 107 Circular St.

Circular Street and the streets adjacent to it were developed by prosperous year-round residents of Saratoga Springs. In the 1830s and 1840s, as the city grew into a center of commercial activity in the region, and an increasingly popular resort destination, successful businessmen who prospered in the local economy eschewed the "society" neighborhood of Franklin Square. Instead, they built gracious houses on Circular Street where they could look down to Putnam Street and Broadway where many of their businesses were located.

The residences in this neighborhood reflect the lifestyle and prosperity of these local merchants in a nationally recognized and somewhat notorious health spa and seasonal resort city. The area burghers hired the builders, and later architects, popular among the city's seasonal society, to design more modest year-round residences. In this neighborhood, you would find the residences of hotel and spa owners, retail merchants, mill owners, and successful builders and contractors who prospered as the resort prospered.

❶ 102 CIRCULAR ST.

Milligan Mansion

1853 Italianate Villa

This residence was built by Colonel Robert J. Milligan, a businessman who specialized in lumber and whose family occupied it until 1944, when Isaac M. Lefkovitz, a doctor, purchased it. Dr. Lefkovitz ran his practice from the house, and even offered it as an overflow for patients during an influenza epidemic that hit Skidmore College students. Among the many lovely aspects of this house is the belvedere, or observatory, on the roof and the wide eaves supported by scroll brackets that are decorated with acanthus leaves. This house has its special place in history because the Daughters of the American Revolution drafted their constitution here. Visitors to the Brooklyn Museum will find the parlor and library from the Milligan Mansion, which were sold intact to the museum.

122 Circular St.   105 Lake Ave.

❷ 108 CIRCULAR ST.

c. 1845 Early Italianate

James Savage, one of the owners of the Congress Hall Hotel, built this grand house and it remained his residence until 1870. After passing through the hands of many owners, it became a 20-room boarding house for the next 80 years or so. During the 1970s, the Saratoga Arts Workshop was located here. As time passed the building fell into disrepair and sections were removed. The house was purchased in the 1980s and was remodeled extensively for use as a summer residence. The house, with its imposing multi-story porch featuring Corinthian columns that span the front and side of the house, is a striking example of a transition in architectural styles. Its design is principally Italianate and yet it retains some of the general look of a Greek Revival design.

❸ 120 CIRCULAR ST.

1903 Colonial Revival

R. Newton Brezee, architect

Designed by prominent architect R. Newton Brezee, 120 Circular St. was built in 1903, probably by William Case, partner in the Saratoga Springs contracting firm Case Brothers. The house was fitted with both gas and electricity and the fireplaces were originally intended for gas logs rather than for coal or wood. It boasts a total of 88 windows. In 1923, the house was sold to Mrs. Marcelle Halligan and her sister, Marguerite, both registered nurses, who operated the Viasana Convalescent Rest Home in the building. In 1946, it became a boarding house, and by 1977, it was known as the Circular Lodge. The house stood vacant for 15 years, abandoned and often vandalized, until the present owners bought the house and restored it as a bed and breakfast. While a combination of many architectural styles, the house is mainly Colonial Revival, with its tripartite door adapted from the Federal and Greek Revival styles. Greek meander, or fretwork, ornamental motifs, polygonal bay, engaged pilasters, dentil cornices, and sidelights contrast with the Queen Anne style semi-circular porch.

❹ 122 CIRCULAR ST.

c. 1858 Italianate, Mansard Roof added later

122 Circular St. was originally built for John Benedict, one of

155 Circular St.

162 Circular St.

Saratoga Springs' affluent figures from the 1840s to 1860s. Mr. Benedict seems to have devoted his entire life to his work in Saratoga Springs but did not enjoy lasting success here. From the upper stories of his house, he could probably look down Caroline Street and view his many businesses. Some of Benedict's properties included a stone house and lumber yard on Putnam Street, a steam mill on Henry Street, another lumber yard on Henry Street, and shops on Putnam Street. Mr. Benedict lost his fortune when his mill caught on fire during construction of the Grand Union Hotel. Embarrassed by his business failure, Benedict moved to Des Moines, Iowa, leaving behind his unique home. Among the interesting architectural details are two towers incorporated into the design of the façade, and the handsome brick detailing beneath the windows on the towers. The beautiful mansard roof, which was added to the house, retains its original ironwork cresting.

{Dr. Grace Swanner}

Born in Albany in 1901, Grace Maguire always knew she wanted to be a doctor. Her parents were not supportive of young Grace's ambitions. She attended college at the New York School for Teachers, graduating in 1923. She went on to study at Columbia University and received a master's degree in 1927. Despite her family's presumed objections, Grace did pre-med coursework at the University of Chicago through 1929 and then entered Albany Medical College. Finally, in 1933, Grace's dream came true and she graduated from Albany Medical College, the only woman in her class. Following an internship in Albany and residency in New Jersey, Dr. Swanner located her practice in general and internal medicine in her home, and for many years she was the only female doctor in Saratoga Springs. In 1936, she joined Dr. Walter McClellan at the Saratoga Spa to assist him in his research on the health effects of the water from the famed springs. Dr. Swanner was also a senior physician at Saratoga Hospital until 1975. After retiring from her practice, she went back to school to earn a degree in fine arts from Skidmore College. In 1988, Dr. Swanner wrote about her experiences working with internationally renowned Dr. McClellan in the book *Saratoga, Queen of the Spas*. Dr. Swanner died in 2000, at the age of 98.

| 206 Regent St.

❺ 137 CIRCULAR ST.

1868 Victorian Cottage

The cottage at 137 Circular St. was most likely built for E.G. Rawson, proprietor of Rawson and Merchant, purveyors of soaps, candles and other sundries. In 1898, Mr. Rawson succeeded his father as head of the S.E.G Rawson Company, pioneer manufacturers of elastic, self-adjusting bandages that were first sold only to the U.S. Army and later became a well-known product. The large brackets massed at key architectural points distinguish this residence.

❻ 105 LAKE AVE.

1885 Victorian Gothic

R. Newton Brezee, architect

The house at 105 Lake Ave. was built on the site of an earlier house. From the 1840s to 1884, the Gleason family owned and operated a farm on the site. In October 1885, Joseph P. Gilson, a lumberman from Georgia, bought the property and contracted with Newton Brezee to design a summer house. Gilson supplied all of the specially selected Georgia pine for the interior of the house. Architecturally, this house is an outstanding example of the Victorian Gothic style of architecture, with a tower designed into the façade of the building that anchors the corner, and lavish detail and ornamentation on the front porches.

❼ 107 LAKE AVE.

c. 1854 Greek Revival

William H. Walton, descendent of Henry Walton who figured prominently in the tourism trade and development of Saratoga Springs in the first half of the 19th century, was likely the first owner of this house. The building is transitional in style; while generally Greek Revival in design, it illustrates definite features of the Italianate Villa style in various ways. Notice, particularly, the asymmetrically placed front entrance and the windows creating four long narrow sections in the façade of the house. The semi-cupola, with its decorative iron cresting, is also indicative of the Italianate style. This house was the home of Dr. Grace Swanner when she began her medical practice in Saratoga Springs in 1936.

❽ 155 CIRCULAR ST.

c. 1884 Victorian Gothic

This house has wonderful detailing, which is particularly elaborate at the tops of the columns and below the eaves of the front porch. The slate roof is striped with scalloped and oblong shingles. And the front-gable apex features an intricate wooden medieval pendant and scrolls.

43 York Ave.

❾ 162 CIRCULAR ST.

c. 1892 Victorian Gothic Stick Style

This structure's highly decorative ornamentation is found in various other styles such as Victorian Gothic and Queen Anne. The ornamentation was mechanically carved, giving the appearance of the heavy-legged furniture of this period. The U-shaped porch has a central pediment over the entranceway and directly above it is a square tower incorporated into the façade with an open area on top. A large turret with a spire-like piece on top caps the tower.

❿ 163 CIRCULAR ST.

1894 Colonial Revival

This beautiful Colonial Revival structure has a bold pediment, alternate rows of staggering shingles and an irregular, multi-paneled sash window. A hexagonal tower is incorporated into the façade. The L- shaped porch has a large pediment over the doorway, again with staggered shingles. There is a small porch on the second floor to the left of the tower. The house was originally built for George Stoddard, a traveling salesman, and his wife, Ella. The Stoddards apparently rented rooms in their home, as Ezra and Ada Gray also resided at 163 Circular St. Ezra had a carriage trimming businesses at 50 Caroline St. and Ada was a dressmaker.

⓫ 173 CIRCULAR ST.

c. 1840 Greek Revival

John and Elizabeth Palmer, owners of a boarding house located at 93 Circular St., built this residence. From 1901 to 1928, it was owned by Edward F. Andrews, the city's deputy assessor. The house is a classic Greek Revival, but has an ornately detailed Victorian Gothic porch. The door has sidelights and a transom typical of the Greek Revival style.

⓬ 172 CIRCULAR ST.

c. 1923 Craftsman

The house at 172 Circular St. is one of the greatest examples of the Craftsman style in Saratoga Springs. Built for Robert Clark, vice president of Clark Textiles, this simple, strong house features fieldstone detailing and wood shingles, and stands in contrast to its more lavish Victorian neighbors. A broad, segmented arch spanning the porch is typical of the Craftsman style that gained popularity in the post-World War I years.

⑬ 43 YORK AVE.

c. 1884 Victorian Gothic

The first owners of this house were William Fitzpatrick, a jockey, and his wife, Ann. At one point, the house was converted into apartments. Now, however, it has been restored to a one-family house, complete with Victorian detailing, especially in the peak of the front gable and on the porch posts.

⑭ 19 MARION PLACE

1899 Richardsonian Queen Anne

R. Newton Brezee, architect

R. Newton Brezee, designed this house for Willis and Abbie Kendrick in 1899. According to that year's city directories, Mr. Kendrick, a pharmacist and manufacturer of "Spruce Remedies," moved from 3 Marion Place to No. 19 in October 1899. The house, which remained in the Kendrick family for almost 100 years, is an outstanding example of Richardsonian Queen Anne style of the late Victorian period in architecture (1880-1895) in transition to the Colonial Revival style. It is a massive stone, brick and shingled 2-story house with a large semi-circular wrapped porch and Richardsonian arches.

⑮ 20 MARION PLACE

1901 Colonial Revival

Once owned by Saratoga Springs mayor Clarence Knapp, this lovely Colonial Revival house features a variety of window types and styles. There are original multi-paned and leaded glass windows still remaining. Worth noting is the arched window on the north side. The porch has been restored to its historic design.

19 Marion Place

173 Circular St.

159 Phila St.

⓰ 26 MARION PLACE

1902 Colonial Revival

26 Marion Place consists of both a main house and a carriage house. A stunning focal point window to the right of the door of the main house has leaded windows on the top. Notice the stained-glass windows on the left side of the house, illuminating the interior stairs. The carriage house has been restored and is now used as a residence. The house was originally built for Harry Crocker, a contractor and dealer in lumber, slate and paint whose shop was at 65 Putnam St.

⓱ 14 TALFORD PLACE

c. 1886 Queen Anne/Romanesque Revival

This building once served as the stables for the Colonial Revival style residence at 181 Phila St.. Architects LaFarge, Warren and Clark designed the carriage house, which featured impressive stone work, an intricate brick walk, and a massive turnstile for automobiles. It has since been converted to residential use.

⓲ 184 PHILA STREET

James House

c. 1865 Italianate and Victorian Gothic

Rufus Dorn, architect (attributed)

This High Victorian Gothic residence is one of the best examples of this style remaining in Saratoga Springs. The entrance to the house is located in a slightly projecting bay that terminates at the roofline with a magnificent four-tiered pagoda rooftop. The unusual gables with verge boards form a Palladian arch arrangement with pointed pendants, behind which is set a small rounded arch attic window. In 1876, Lewis W. James, vice president of the Vichy Spring Company, purchased the house. The house remained in the James family for 90 years. During the 1990s, the building was extensively renovated.

⓳ 181 PHILA ST.

c. 1888 Colonial Revival

J. Townsend Lansing of Albany was the original owner of this house and it remained in his ownership until 1920. For the next 40 years, the house was a summer residence, a "cottage" as described in the Saratoga Springs city directory, for the Payne and Helen Whitney family. In the 1960s and early 1970s, the house was the summer

150 Phila St.

residence of Joan Whitney Payson, who was an owner of the New York Mets baseball team. Of particular note are the steeply pitched roof of irregular shape, the unusual dormers and a front-facing gable end. Other identifying features include cutaway bay windows, the asymmetrical façade, and a porch extending along more than one side.

⓴ 180 PHILA ST.
c. 1840 Greek Revival
John Benedict built the simple cottage at 180 Phila St. for J.H. Loveland, a painter. Mr. Benedict, a prominent Saratoga Springs entrepreneur, was noted for having assisted the men who worked for him to obtain homes for themselves on easy terms, generally payable in work.

㉑ 159 PHILA ST.
Waterbury House
c. 1872 Italianate
159 Phila St., long known as the Waterbury House, was built for Edward Waterbury, a watchmaker and jeweler whose shop was at 136 Broadway. The house, which stayed in the Waterbury family until the 1930s, is of the Italianate style with a one-story porch and double-arched doors. Other identifying details include a deep cornice and fancy supporting brackets, ornamental window caps and side-by-side windows. The square columns on the porch have the so-called "flamingo knees" typical of the Victorian era in American architecture.

㉒ 150 PHILA ST.
1868 Second Empire
Attributed to Rufus Dorn, architect
150 Phila St. was originally the home of Benjamin Franklin Judson, and his wife, Elizabeth. Judson was a printer who came to Saratoga Springs in 1855 and who left his mark on city and county politics. Mr. Judson began publishing the weekly *Temperance Helper,* which he renamed *The Saratogian* on Jan. 1, 1856. Nathaniel Bartlett Sylvester, in his *History of Saratoga County* (Samuel T. Wiley and Winfield Scott Garner. 1893.) describes Mr. Judson as a "zealous Republican" who was active in the party from its formation in 1856. In 1861, Mr.

| 184 Phila St.

Judson joined the 77th Regiment of the New York State Volunteers, which he had helped establish, and became senior captain of the regiment. In the spring of 1862, he returned home having resigned his commission because of an injury. In 1868, soon after Ulysses S. Grant was elected President of the United States, Mr. Judson was appointed postmaster of Saratoga Springs, a position he held for many years.

In 1902, the house was purchased by Dr. George Scott Towne, and remained in the Towne family until 1954. Dr. Towne, a prominent physician, had his offices in the basement.

150 Phila St. is a wonderful example of the Second Empire style. The mansard roof and the heavily decorated projecting dormers typify this style. The entire house is decorated with machine-cut ornamentation. The design is attributed to architect Rufus Dorn because of the unique second-floor dormer windows. Dorn was a Saratoga Springs architect who also worked in Rochester and Los Angeles. When he moved to Rochester, he took with him a letter of reference signed by B.F. Judson, and several other prominent Saratoga Springs businessmen.

㉓ 115 CIRCULAR ST.
1895 Colonial Revival
Harry M. Levengston, proprietor and builder of the Saratoga Baths, built the house at 115 Circular St., which is a fine example of Colonial Revival architecture in Saratoga Springs. Worth noting on the south side chimney is a plaque decorated with a garland in relief and applied to the chimney wall.

㉔ 27 LAFAYETTE ST.
1902 Colonial Revival
Now a single-family house, 27 Lafayette St. was originally the private garage of Harry Levengston, builder and proprietor of the Saratoga Baths, who lived at 115 Circular St. A periodical of the time referred to Mr. Levengston as an "automobilist and enthusiast of the popular sport." He could often be found in his garage working as a mechanic on his cars and working with his extensive collection of guns and rifles. On the first floor of the tower on the northeast corner of the house, the original steel turntable used for turning the cars around has been retained.

㉕ 15 LAFAYETTE ST.
c. 1880 Queen Anne
The first owner of this residence was William P. Lewis, a clothier. He remained until 1893, when William P. Tarrant of Tarrant and Ingmire

Plumbers purchased it. Prominent Queen Anne features in this house include the asymmetrical façade, the use of both shingles and clapboard siding, and the prominent bay window.

㉖ 14 LAFAYETTE ST.

c. 1835 Greek Revival

The house at 14 Lafayette St. is built into a hillside, three stories are visible on the front of the house, while only two are visible in the rear. This house was built soon after Lafayette Street was laid out. It is one of the earliest surviving modest houses in the city and retains a remarkable amount of early decorative detail. The front door has original classic Greek Revival tall double panels, flanking pilasters and side lights. The 6 (panes) over 6 divided light windows are replicas of the originals. The Italianate porch, which reaches the second floor on the front, is a later addition.

㉗ 60 HENRY ST.

c. 1858 Victorian Vernacular

The residence at 60 Henry St. is a fine example of the Italianate Victorian style with its asymmetrical design, decorative wooden window brackets, two-story bay window and one-story porch with rounded arches. This style, with its simple detailing, became popular in the 1840s and 1850s. The Italianate Victorian style swept the nation because of its flexibility. The exterior walls could be shaped to fit the requirements of the interior and the style could be embellished or restrained to meet individual tastes. Daniel H. Main, a prominent carpenter and contractor, was the builder and original owner of the house. He leased it to craftsmen who worked in the building industry.

㉘ 61 LAKE AVE.

Lake Avenue Armory

1889 Richardsonian Romanesque

Isaac Perry, architect

The Armory, which now houses the New York State Military Museum, was designed by Isaac Perry, who was also one of the architects for the New York State Capitol building in Albany. Through his work on the state Capitol, Perry developed a mastery of what he called H.H. Richardson's American Romanesque style. The Lake Avenue Armory, with its rock-faced stone, red brick and terra cotta walls, Assyrian arches, and carefully balanced asymmetrical elements, is a strong example of this style of architecture. The façade of the Armory is beautifully decorated with carved terra cotta sculpture; particularly noteworthy is the lion's head to the south of the main tower.

161 Lake Ave., Armory

㉙ 129 CIRCULAR ST.

Jumel Cottage

1832 Greek Revival

The house at 129 Circular is very similar to its neighbor, and was likely built by the same contractor, John Hodgman. Worth noting are its four square columns, which were less expensive to build than the round fluted columns more typical in the Greek Revival style. This house is famous more for its inhabitants than its architecture. This was the home of Madame Eliza Jumel.

㉚ 127 CIRCULAR ST.

Hodgman House

c. 1839 Greek Revival with later modifications

This house and the one next door, the Jumel house, were built by John Hodgman, a blacksmith and house builder, and his wife Zilpha. In 1900, the residence became a rental property, owned by Sidney and Minerva Rickard. Mrs. Rickard died in 1924 and left the house to the New England Congregational Church. The church used it as housing for the next 50 years. Originally a vernacular Greek Revival house, 127 Circular has undergone extensive renovation over its life. Some of the Greek influences are evident in the transom and sidelights surrounding the door and in the frieze band below the eaves; the Palladian window in the front dormer and the hipped roof illustrate the Colonial Revival period changes.

㉛ 107 CIRCULAR ST.

First Church of Christ Scientist

c. 1850 Greek Revival with a Colonial Revival porch

From 1876 to 1890, the house at 107 Circular was the home of J. Augustus Smith, a watchmaker and jeweler whose shop was located at 358 Broadway. In 1891, the first Christian Science Society in Saratoga Springs was established. In 1930, the present First Church of Christ Scientist was organized and the new church building was dedicated. Over the years, this Greek Revival building has undergone a number of renovations, including the addition of a Victorian door and a Colonial Revival porch with its classic Ionic columns.

129 Circular St.

{Madame Eliza Jumel}

Eliza Jumel remains one of the most talked-about women in Saratoga's history. Although she was only a summer resident, her scandalous life is worth recounting. Born in Providence, Rhode Island, to a prostitute mother, Eliza left for New York City to seek a better life for herself, becoming the mistress of New York City businessman Stephen Jumel. It is said that in order to convince Jumel to marry her, Eliza feigned imminent death. Talk of Eliza's origins reached Jumel, and to escape scandal, the couple traveled to France, where he introduced her to the elite of Paris. The Jumel fortune dwindled and Eliza returned to New York, leaving Jumel in France to rebuild his business. Madame Jumel took New York by storm and through a number of clever real estate and business deals was once again a wealthy woman. Unfortunately for Jumel, his wife had surreptitiously transferred all of his assets to her name.

After Jumel's death, Madame Jumel agreed to marry Aaron Burr, a long-time admirer. It is thought that Madame Jumel married Burr for his name and social status, and Burr pursued Madame Jumel for her money. Theirs was not a happy union, and ultimately Madame Jumel divorced Burr, who died shortly after.

She aspired to be embraced by New York's social elite, which may be why Madame Jumel chose to summer in Saratoga Springs. She could often be found maneuvering her carriage to the front in the daily parade of society matrons. Madame Jumel's ambitions were noted by the locals who attempted to embarrass her by mimicking her elaborate dress and affected attitude. After a particularly harsh episode, Madame Jumel's presence in Saratoga Springs waned. Nonetheless, it is the name of Madame Jumel we remember among the many society women who have graced the city through the years.

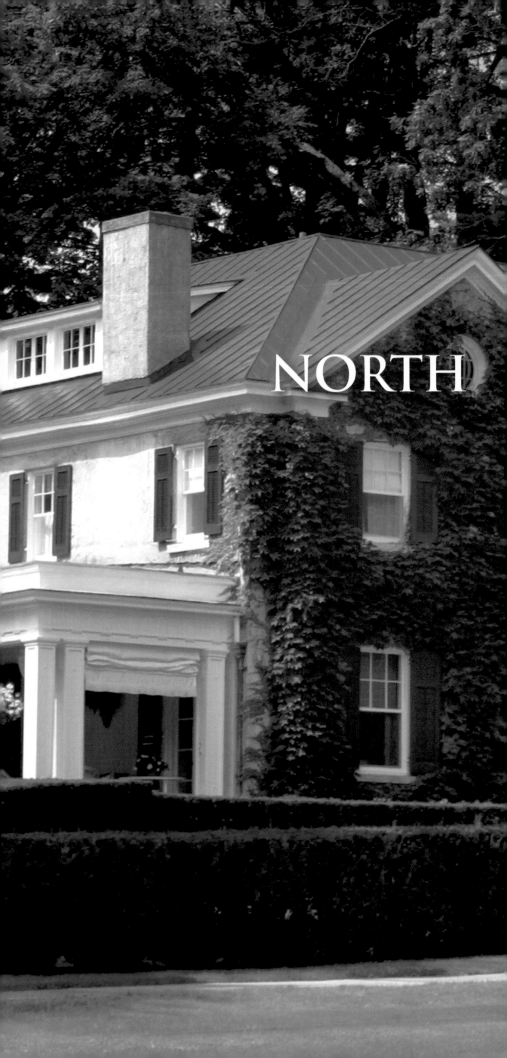

NORTH

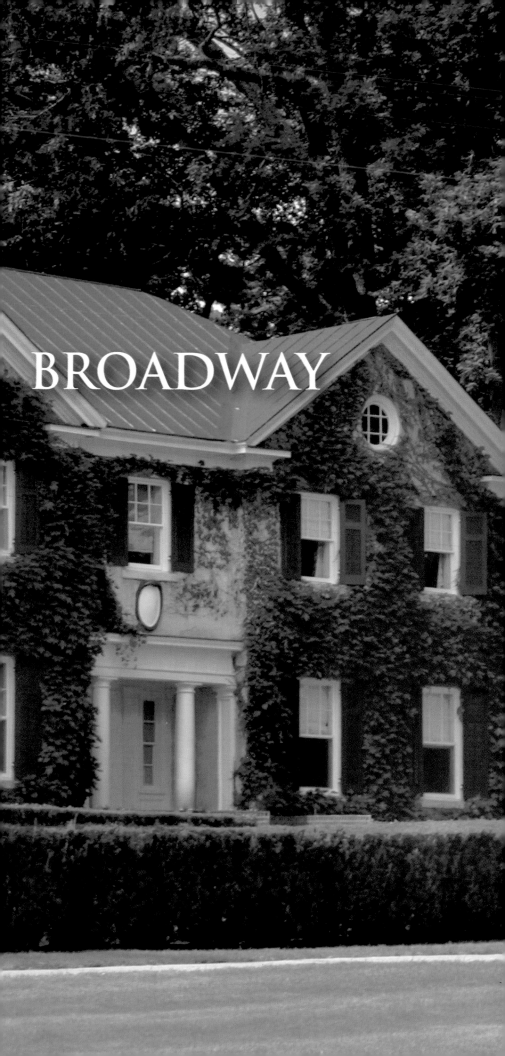

BROADWAY

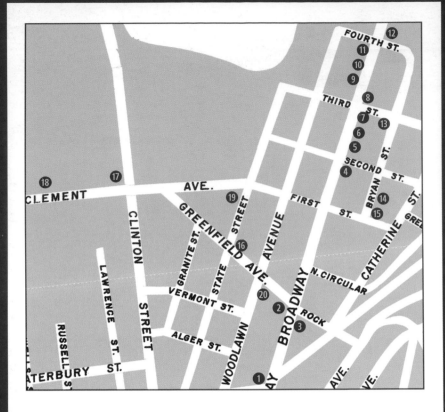

TOUR DETAILS

Distance: 2.2 miles

Steps: 4,141

Time: Approximately 55 minutes

Terrain: Some steady gradual inclines

Directions: Start at Broadway and Rt 50. North to Fourth St. East on Fourth St. to Bryant St. South on Bryant St. to First St. West on First St. to Broadway. Cross Broadway and west on Greenfield Ave. to Clement Ave. West on Clement Ave. to Clinton St. Reverse and back to Broadway. South on Broadway to the beginning.

TOUR HIGHLIGHTS

❶ 563 North Broadway

❷ 601 North Broadway

❸ 632 North Broadway

❹ 718 North Broadway

❺ 720 North Broadway

❻ 722 North Broadway

❼ 748 North Broadway

❽ 760 North Broadway

❾ 779 North Broadway

❿ 791 North Broadway

⓫ 795 North Broadway

⓬ 950 North Broadway

⓭ 57 Bryan St.

⓮ 8 Bryan St.

⓯ 6 Bryan St.

⓰ 45 Greenfield Ave.

⓱ 245 Clinton St.

⓲ 10 Carriage House Lane

⓳ 1 Clement Ave.

⓴ 22 Greenfield Ave.

$\mathcal{N}$orth Broadway is a beautiful tree-lined avenue, a gracious extension of the city's main thoroughfare. Broadway was originally laid out by two of the town's best-known resident developers, Henry Walton and Gideon Putnam, during the early 1800s. When the Saratoga and Schenectady Railroad came to town, bringing with it more visitors, as well as permanent residents, the city began to grow. By 1854, North Broadway had been constructed and became a residential area, while the southern area bustled with commercial ventures. During the 1880s, building on North Broadway took off. Magnificent houses on large lots were constructed for people who had earned their fortunes in the post-Civil War era. These residences also had barns, stables or carriage houses located on service streets parallel to Broadway so household goods could be discreetly delivered to the houses.

Around 1900, at the height of its popularity, Saratoga Springs drew influential, elegant and scandalous individuals from New York City. These movers and shakers rented houses on North Broadway for the summer to enjoy the races and gambling Saratoga Springs had to offer. It was a mark of status to stay in the best houses on North Broadway. At the same time, influential industrialists who had struck it rich, many of who came from Troy, New York, built summer "cottages" on North Broadway.

Although Saratoga Springs was a booming city during the late 19th and early 20th centuries, it fell out of fashion for a variety of reasons and many of these grand houses fell into disrepair. Today, however, private investment and preservation activism has saved many of these enduring examples of a variety of building styles, echoing the whims and whimsy of times long past. In recent years, interest in Saratoga Springs has blossomed and homeowners, many of whom are still "summer people," have lovingly restored their houses to their original beauty. A number of estates have been divided and sold in parts; their carriage houses, which once served the grand houses, are now spectacular residences in their own right. Even barns have been turned into private residences. The former service streets have now

563 North Broadway

become integral parts of vibrant neighborhoods. A stroll along North Broadway and its neighboring side streets will offer examples of all types of architecture existing in the city.

❶ 563 NORTH BROADWAY
1884 Queen Anne

This house was built for Dr. Adelbert Hewitt, a well-known Saratoga Springs physician and surgeon, who lived here with his family from 1884 to1904. In 1964, the Salvation Army purchased the house. Under their ownership, many alterations were made that obscured the characteristic details and porches. In 2003, the house was restored, its beauty uncovered, and it is now the headquarters of a local builder with luxury apartments on the top two floors. This building received a New York State Preservation Award in 2004.

❷ 601 NORTH BROADWAY
1885 Queen Anne

The first owner of this house was James Pardue, owner of the China Hall at 452-454 Broadway and The Algonquin apartments, followed by industrialist Daniel W. Coon of Troy, and later by Julia Morrison of Troy. After World War II, the house became part of the Beverly Manor hotel. The house is constructed of painted brick veneer and has an interesting roof line; also of note is the stucco decoration in the projecting attic gable. The Colonial Revival details in the first floor bay and the porte-cochere are evidence of the individual tastes of the various owners.

❸ 632 NORTH BROADWAY
Sidney A. Rickard House
1884 Queen Anne

The men and women who first owned this house were quite influential in the Saratoga Springs scene. The house's original owner, Sidney A. Rickard, came to Saratoga Springs and opened an interior decorating business and was known for "his exquisite taste and judgment as to color and effects." He became "the" expert in interior design and his talents were much sought after throughout the region. He sold his design business in 1886. The same year, he joined the

G.F. Harvey Co., a pharmaceutical manufacturing company based in Saratoga Springs. Sidney's wife, Minerva L. Rickard, left a strong legacy in Saratoga Springs as one of the founders of The Saratoga Hospital, the only hospital of its day founded by women. Other notable Saratogians including, Webster C. Moriarta and his wife, Bertha, later owned this house. Mr. Moriarta was the president of the Saratoga Vichy Spring Company. Worth noting are the multi-paned windows in the upper story and the fanciful Victorian gable decorations, along with the massive chimneys.

❹ 718 NORTH BROADWAY
"The Evergreens" Winsor B. French House
1865 Italianate Villa

This house was the residence of Winsor B. French, a high-profile Saratoga Springs attorney who was a partner in the Pond, French, and Brackett law firm. The house was built in the fashionable Italianate Villa style, with a square tower built into the facade. Different owners, each of whom put their own stamp on the building, have added elements of a variety of styles. For example, the lovely porch is an example of Colonial Revival architecture.

❺ 720 NORTH BROADWAY
Ellis Cottage
1885 Shingle
Edward Clark and Charles Berg, architects

This shingle house was designed by prominent New York City architects Edward Clark and Charles Berg, and constructed for the Ellis family, owners of the American Locomotive Works and the Ellis Steamship line. Continuous wood shingles envelop the building and this unique wraparound effect is carried through on the interior of the house as rooms flow into one another. The interior of this cheerful,

720 North Broadway

722 North Broadway

791 North Broadway

welcoming home was used as one of the foreboding backdrops of the 1981 film, *Ghost Story.*

❻ 722 NORTH BROADWAY
Kilmer House
1887 Queen Anne
S. Gifford Slocum, architect
This lovely Queen Anne style house has a wraparound porch in rough, rock-faced stone. The masonry reflects the influence of Henry Hobson Richardson, one of the most influential and well-respected architects of his day. Richardson was one of the designers of the state Capitol building in Albany. Incorporating the whims and tastes of the owners, the house has two distinct towers, one with a bulbous roof, the other conical, and other architectural elements including a gable, a minaret, Stick-style detailing in wood, terra cotta decoration and Tiffany stained-glass windows. Like its neighbor, this house was also used as a setting in the 1981 film *Ghost Story.*

❼ 748 NORTH BROADWAY
1880 Victorian Gothic
This cheery house is modest in comparison to its neighbors and features charming cottage-style ornamentation, including gingerbread woodwork on the gable and a welcoming porch that invites relaxation. A great example of the tastes of the day, this house is similar in style to a house found in the former Methodist camp in nearby Round Lake.

❽ 760 NORTH BROADWAY
1906 Colonial Revival
The house at 760 North Broadway is a classic example of the Colonial Revival style, with features of the Georgian Colonial, the Federal and the Greek Revival styles. The 760 North Broadway house was built during a period in which Saratoga Springs was losing its national significance as a resort town and summer residences were being built for people who lived near Saratoga Springs. William Lord Hall, a successful shirt manufacturer from Troy, built this magnificent Colonial Revival. In 1965, Stephen B. Wilson donated the house to Skidmore College, which was in the process of building its new campus on the adjacent Woodlawn Park. Skidmore's president,

779 North Broadway

Joseph C. Palamountain and his wife, Anne, lived in the house through 1987.

This splendid house is an example of eclectic architectural tastes. Its prominent entranceway is marked by a classic Greek Revival portico supported by ornate Corinthian columns. Other interesting details include Victorian asymmetry and bay windows, a Queen Anne chimney, and Federal-style fanlights. A Colonial Revival carriage house and pergola are also on the property. After sitting empty for nearly eight years, the house was purchased in 1994 and was extensively renovated.

❾ 779 NORTH BROADWAY

1882 Queen Anne with Elizabethan and Jacobean details
For a visitor to Saratoga Springs in the 1880s, the place to stay in town was the United States Hotel on Broadway. William Gage, one of its owners, built the striking residence at 779 Broadway in 1881. There is a picturesque quality to the house; its design is reminiscent of English Victorian rather than American. With a majestic balcony, tile roof, and rounded dormers, the house hints of a time and places long ago and far away. The façade is covered with ivy, which gives a hint of mystery. Recent additions to the house were made in 1988. The

{ SARATOGA IN THE MOVIES }

Homes and neighborhoods across Saratoga Springs have provided the setting for a number of films, including:

- His Last Dollar (1914)
- The Racing Strain (1918)
- Saratoga (1937)
- The Homestretch (1947)
- Ghost Story (1981)
- Billy Bathgate (1991)
- The Horse Whisperer (1998)
- The Time Machine (2002)
- Nate Dogg (2003)
- Seabiscuit (2003)

760 North Broadway

circular front porch, and the addition behind it, introduces strong horizontal elements to the house, contrasting with and balancing the verticality of the original design.

⑩ 791 NORTH BROADWAY
c. 1895 Colonial Revival
Lucy Skidmore Scribner, founder of Skidmore College and widow of J. Blair Scribner (of the Scribner publishing family), purchased the house from Walter H. and Rhoby Marvin Bryant in 1897. A classic Colonial Revival house, its most outstanding features include the gambrel roof, which faces the street, delicate columns on the porch, and large Palladian windows.   In the early 1900s, Mrs. Scribner added the porte-cochere; the upper sun porch that she termed "the nest" in her diaries, which was renovated in 2004; the stained-glass windows; and a sizeable back addition. Skidmore College received the house upon Mrs. Scribner's death in 1931, exchanged it for a house on the old campus (46 Circular St., near Congress Park) in 1937, and reacquired it in 1964. In 1987, it became the official residence of the president of Skidmore College.

⑪ 795 NORTH BROADWAY
Red Stone Villa
1886 Queen Anne
S. Gifford Slocum, architect
In 1886, houses designed by S. Gifford Slocum were highly desirable, and this house is a truly fine example of a Slocum design. The owner of this house was Eli Clinton Clark, owner of a successful lumber business and the Clark Mills. Like some of its neighbors, Red Stone Villa has several elements that echo the influence of famed architect, Henry Hobson Richardson. The materials used in construction of this house are intentionally rustic to suggest an appreciation of nature. The pink and red sandstone has a rough-hewn texture, there are terra cotta tiles and colored mortar with rounded cement joints, and the cast terra cotta porch columns are a particularly wonderful detail on this magnificent house.

⑫ 950 NORTH BROADWAY
Surrey Inn
c.1920 English Cottage

795 North Broadway

This house, built by New York stockbroker E. Clarence Jones, was originally known as the Broadview Lodge. The grand estate was modeled after an English country squire's home. The house was situated at the center of the estate that included a superintendent's cottage, stone farm building and garage. Its charm comes from stucco walls and a slate roof. Innovative in its day, the house had what was described as a "vapor" heating system. After Jones' death in 1926, the house changed hands a number of times. In the late 1940s, it became the Brown School for Boys, then a private hotel used by friends of thoroughbred horse owners during racing season, and later as the exclusive Surrey Inn. Skidmore College acquired the Surrey in 1967 and today it is used as a faculty lounge, alumni guesthouse and the setting for many college meetings.

⓭ 57 BRYAN ST.
Charles Cooke Lester Carriage House
1880 Victorian Gothic
This carriage house was built about 1880 for the home of Charles Cooke Lester at 754 Broadway. It was converted into a private residence in 1975. The exterior echoes the Victorian Gothic lines of the main house, with the high pitch of its roof and the pointed gables of its dormer windows. Details of the former carriage house, the stall dividers, a water trough and a bridle rack have all been incorporated into the renovated structure.

{LUCY SKIDMORE SCRIBNER}

Lucy, the wife of New York City publisher John Blair Scribner, felt the women of Saratoga Springs needed additional options when choosing their paths in life. She formed the Young Women's Industrial Club in 1903, which was located in the shingled building at 153 Regent Street. This club offered courses in sewing, cooking and a variety of practical skills. In 1911, Lucy acquired the former Temple Grove Seminary on Circular Street where the Skidmore School of Arts was formed. The school evolved into Skidmore College for Women in 1915 and was chartered by the state of New York in 1922. The college initially offered courses in nursing, liberal arts, fine arts, home economics, health and physical education and secretarial science. Lucy's work changed the lives of countless young women.

1718 North Broadway

⓮ 8 BRYAN ST.

1879 Victorian Vernacular

Built in 1879, its first owner was Annanias Boyce, a working-class man who made a living as a watchman, a policeman and, finally, a deputy sheriff. The house has typical architectural details of houses in Saratoga Springs during the 1870s, including the bracketed porch and rounded brick window caps.

⓯ 6 BRYAN ST.

c.1931 Colonial Revival

Not all who lived along North Broadway were prosperous members of Saratoga's elite society. Some of the area's residents were working class, as was the case with the residents of this lot. During the 1920s, this location was the site of The Coakley Riding Academy. It is believed that some of Saratoga's first polo ponies were boarded here. The original building that stood on this site was demolished in 1932 and a new barn was erected in its place, perhaps by Frank Williams who lived at 4 Bryan St.. In 1985, the barn was converted into a private residence.

⓰ 45 GREENFIELD AVE.

The Home of the Good Shepherd

1900 Colonial Revival

Affiliated with the Episcopal Church, The Home of the Good Shepherd, an adult home for women, was founded between 1866 and 1869 and operated in this location from 1900 until 2004. Among its founders were Mrs. John Gibson, wife of the Rector of Bethesda Episcopal Church, and several parishioners. The building, with its multi-story porches, was designed to be an attractive and secure residence for women and was built largely through donations from the public. It is another example of women in Saratoga Springs taking a leadership role in creating positive social change.

⓱ 245 CLINTON ST.

Annandale Mansion

c.1885 Romanesque Revival/Queen Anne

S. Gifford Slocum, architect

The Annandale is a powerful assertion of the Richardsonian Queen Anne style. Slocum designed a massive house with a myriad of details. The façade is composed of a central bay with rounded corners and a gable roof flanked by a 3-story round tower on the left and an angled, projecting roof dormer on the right. The house was the home of Daniel Shields Lathrop, whose daughter, Aimee Lathrop Hanson, was active in the founding of Saratoga Hospital. A later owner was Harry K. Thaw, a millionaire playboy who was convicted in 1906 of the shocking murder of Stanford White, a noted architect with the firm McKim, Mead and White. Thaw had discovered that his wife, Evelyn Nesbit, had been White's mistress. In 1970, the Annandale Mansion was condemned by the city of Saratoga Springs as an uninhabitable and unsafe structure. Fortunately, the building was saved by converting it to apartments.

⑱ 10 CARRIAGE HOUSE LANE

Carriage House for Annandale Mansion

c.1885 Queen Anne

S. Gifford Slocum, architect

This beautiful 7,000-square-foot Queen Anne style structure originally served as the carriage house for the Annandale Mansion at 245 Clinton St. Prominent Saratoga Springs architect S. Gifford Slocum designed both the house and the carriage house for Daniel Shields Lathrop around 1885. When the building served as a carriage house, there were two floors of usable space. The large windows on the second floor were originally hayloft doors opened by rope pulleys. Between 1980 and 1987, the house underwent major interior renovations as it was converted into a house to meet the needs of a modern family. There have been no structural changes to the house, however, and much of the original woodwork is intact.

⑲ 1 CLEMENT AVE.

Cluett House

c.1885 Queen Anne/Shingle Style

1 Clement Ave. was built as a summer cottage for a successful Troy shirt manufacturer, George B. Cluett. Cluett came to America in 1854 at the age of 16 in pursuit of the American dream. His aspirations were met as he rose through the ranks in the firm of Maulin & Bigelow, manufacturers of men's collars, becoming a partner in 1861. Cluett assumed ownership of the firm two years later and invited his brothers to join him in forming George B. Cluett Brothers and Company. The Romanesque arches and rock-faced stone used in this building show the influence of Henry Hobson Richardson on American architecture. The round tower built into the façade is one of the interesting elements of this building; inside the tower is a staircase. The fish-scale shingles add texture to the building and provide a contrast to the heavy stone work on the first story.

⑳ 22 GREENFIELD AVE.

S. Gifford Slocum House, Walter Butler House

1886 Queen Anne

S. Gifford Slocum, architect

This large asymmetrical Queen Anne house is over 9,000 square feet and has more than 20 rooms. The variety of shapes and materials,

1 Surrey Inn

245 Clinton St.

8 Bryan St.

and the rough cut stone foundation, are typical of the work of S. Gifford Slocum. Of particular note are the three different types of shingles used on the house. The house has been owned at one point or another by a number of Saratoga's notables. The first residents were S. Gifford Slocum and his mother, Phoebe. Later, it became the home of Walter P. Butler, the first mayor of Saratoga Springs when the village became a city in 1915. An intriguing local legend has it that he comes back to "visit" residents. Another famous tenant was actress Lillian Russell, who with her friend, Diamond Jim Brady, spent summers attending the races and enjoying the gaming Saratoga Springs had to offer.

748 North Broadway

BROADWAY AND

DOWNTOWN

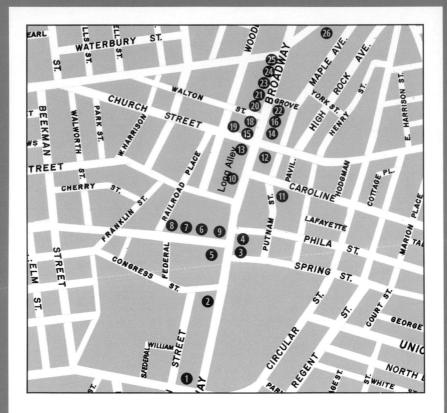

TOUR DETAILS

Distance: 1.5 miles

Steps: 2,933

Time: Approximately 40 minutes

Terrain: Some steady gradual inclines

Directions: Start at corner of W. Circular St. and Broadway. North on Broadway to Caroline St. East on Caroline St. to Putnam St. Reverse. West on Caroline St. to Broadway. Continue North on Broadway to Firehouse. Reverse. South on Broadway to Visitor Center.

TOUR HIGHLIGHTS

❶ 231 Broadway

❷ 297 Broadway

❸ 358 Broadway

❹ 360 Broadway

❺ 39 Washington St.

❻ 24 Washington St.

❼ 41 Washington St.

❽ 45 Washington St.

❾ 365 Broadway

❿ 437 Broadway

⓫ 24 Caroline St.

⓬ 456-470 Broadway

⓭ 473 Broadway

⓮ 474 Broadway

⓯ 475 Broadway

⓰ 480-494 Broadway

⓱ 487 Broadway
(not on map)

⓲ 495 Broadway

⓳ 41 Long Alley

⓴ 505 Broadway

㉑ 509 Broadway

㉒ 504-520 Broadway

㉓ 511 Broadway

㉔ 517 Broadway

㉕ 543 Broadway

㉖ 123 Maple Ave.

BROADWAY

The "Broad Way" of Saratoga Springs was originally laid out in 1805 by Gideon Putnam, a prosperous entrepreneur and landholder. Connecting the Upper Village, near what is now High Rock Park, and the Lower Village, near Congress Park, Broad Way was a wide strip meant to serve as the center of the rapidly growing town. Putnam's daughter, Phila, and granddaughter, Caroline, are memorialized in the streets running east from Broadway.

In 1832, the railroad came to town. The Saratoga and Schenectady Railroad arrived at the station just west of Broadway, bringing with it tourists hoping to enjoy the waters of Saratoga Springs' famous springs. Grand hotels and boarding houses were built to accommodate the increasing number of visitors. Broadway grew into a thriving city center with shops and townhouses popping up along the side streets to the east and west of this thoroughfare.

Throughout the 19th century, but particularly in its latter half, Saratoga Springs was the place to be for America's fashionable. Stoddard's 1884 guide touted the city as having "accommodations for the rich and the poor, the old and the young, steady and giddy, wise or foolish, fast or staid, rough or cultivated — all are welcome, for Saratoga is one vast caravansary, every house a hotel, and every resident glad to see the summer's company…." Summer visitors flocked to the town by carriage, train and steamboat to the Queen of the Spas to benefit from the curative waters, dabble with other fashionable folks and enjoy the racing. The term "Saratoga Trunk" was coined during this era to poke fun at the enormous trunks stuffed with hordes of elaborate dresses the tourists brought with them on their restful holiday. These trunks could be seen being dragged through the rail station and city streets as the travel-weary made their way to their accommodations.

The first garage for automobiles in Saratoga Springs was established in 1909, signaling the emergence of a more mobile society, one whose members were no longer in need of large, gracious hotels that could accommodate them for an entire season. Auto camps and

504-520 Broadway, the Algonquin

motor courts beckoned. During the 1920s and 1930s, the casinos and nightclubs for which Saratoga Springs had become known were controlled mostly by organized crime. The decline of Saratoga Springs had begun. The race track closed for a short time during World War II — long enough to dim the lights on Saratoga Springs' Broadway. Then, in 1952, as a result of U.S. Senator Estes Kefauver's Congressional investigations, Governor Thomas Dewey launched a widespread probe into gambling in Saratoga County. Saratoga Springs went into a sharp decline. Gloom and doom prevailed in the city. By the end of the 1950s, many of the famous hotels were gone, lost to fire or to the wrecking ball. The city's residents were sure the final blow had been dealt to the town and that the economy of the area would not survive.

Through the efforts of dedicated, energetic young men and women, and with the enthusiastic support of Governor Nelson Rockefeller, beginning in the 1960s, Saratoga Springs experienced a renaissance. Committed community members worked to craft a "Plan of Action" that would encourage investment in their city and bring back the thriving resort town of years past. In the mid-1970s, volunteer crews could be found planting new trees along Broadway. Grassroots efforts to save historic structures from inappropriate development protected important cultural resources. The Adirondack Trust Company, the hometown bank, played a key role by helping property owners finance necessary rehabilitation projects in neighborhoods all across the city.

Over the last 40 years, the grand 19th century architecture lining Broadway has been restored and new hotels, restaurants, nightclubs and shops have moved in. Today a visitor to downtown Saratoga Springs experiences the excitement of a lively, vibrant urban center on Broadway, where people come to shop, dine, work and live.

❶ 231 BROADWAY
Inn at Saratoga
1843 Greek Revival
The Inn at Saratoga was originally the Everett House, a boarding house. As described in Stoddard's 1884 guide, Saratoga Springs'

boarding houses were "first class… and unique in everything, and unapproached in excellence anywhere else." The Inn is the sole survivor of four hotels that once stood on this block, and is Saratoga Springs' longest continually operating inn. Over the years, it has hosted a "wealthy and cultured class of guests" who visited Saratoga to partake of the waters. A mix of architectural styles can be seen in the Inn; the original brick front is designed in the Greek Revival style and the cantilevered gable on the fourth floor is an example of the High Victorian Gothic style.

② 297 BROADWAY
Heritage Area Visitor Center
1915 Beaux-Arts
William Orr Ludlow and Charles S. Peabody, architects
This building, an architectural gem, was originally built as a trolley station for the Hudson Valley Railroad. Summer visitors could catch the trolley to take them out to the Saratoga Springs Reservation, now the Saratoga Spa State Park. When, in the 1940s, the building became a drink hall, supplying visitors with samples of Saratoga's mineral water. In the years since, the building has had many uses. In the 1980s, the city of Saratoga Springs transformed the building into its Visitor Center, where tourists can find information about the city's history and current happenings. The interior space is reminiscent of classical Roman buildings; the main hall features barrel-vaulted ceilings and curved apse-like spaces at either end. Displays of Saratoga Springs history, including murals by Cyril Chapman depicting scenes of Saratoga Springs, can also be found here.

③ 358 BROADWAY
Granite Palace
1880 Romanesque Revival
S. Gifford Slocum, architect
This commercial building sits on the former site of Rockwell Putnam's

231 Broadway, Inn at Saratoga

139 Washington St., Bethesda Episcopal Church

home. (Rockwell was one of Gideon Putnam's sons.) Of note are a stone-faced arcade that spans the first two floors and the stone arches that are used to indicate the entrance, which is off-center.

❹ 360 BROADWAY

1867 Victorian Commercial

Built in 1867, this building has had a variety of occupants. It has been a hardware store, *The Daily Saratogian*, the Commercial National Bank, an insurance company and a retail clothing shop. The building is a fine example of Victorian commercial architecture of the era. The recessed bay windows and the flat-arched, keystone-accented windows are original to the bank. Probably the most interesting and significant element of the building is its four-inch-thick carved walnut door. This masterpiece of late 19th century craftsmanship is graced with roped moldings, mostly hand-carved, around its perfectly arched top.

❺ 39 WASHINGTON ST.

Bethesda Episcopal Church

1842 Gothic Revival, 1887 Romanesque Revival façade

Richard Upjohn, architect

The church was originally designed by one of the Victorian era's most important architects, Richard Upjohn of New York City. Among Upjohn's more well-known commissions is Trinity Church on Wall Street. Trinity Church and Bethesda Church were the first Gothic Revival churches built in America. Upjohn's design of Bethesda Church featured an asymmetrical façade with a battlemented balustrade and stone horizontal bands separating the stories. In 1887, A. Page Brown was hired to redesign the church. He shifted the tower from the right to the left corner of the church, so that it stood clear of the Grand Union Hotel, which wrapped around the church. At the front of the church, above the main doors, are three stained-glass panels designed by Louis Comfort Tiffany. These fine examples of American stained glass from the late 19th century were a gift to the church from Spencer and Katrina Trask.

❻ 24 WASHINGTON ST.

Universal Preservation Hall

1871 High Victorian Gothic

This building is one of the earliest examples of High Victorian Gothic architecture in the United States. The church was built in 1871 to host the annual Methodist Conference and the local congregation on a weekly basis. In 1976, the Universal Baptist Church congregation purchased the church from the Methodist Church. Over the years, the building fell into disrepair and was condemned. In the 1990s, the Saratoga Springs Preservation Foundation took on the project of

437 Broadway

working with the congregation to stabilize the building and save it
from being demolished. Out of this effort a new organization, the
Universal Preservation Hall, was formed to adapt this majestic church
to serve as a community performing arts center, a convention and
special-events space, and as the sanctuary of the Universal Baptist
Church.

❼ 41 WASHINGTON ST.
Bethesda Episcopal Church Parish House
c.1860 High Victorian Italianate
Albert S. Washburn built this residence during the 1860s. It
operated as a boarding house until the early 1900s, when Spencer and
Katrina Trask purchased it and donated the building to the Bethesda
Episcopal Church for use as its parish house.

❽ 45 WASHINGTON ST.
First Baptist Church
1855 Greek Revival
This splendid church was built on land given by Gideon Putnam
for a house of worship "not less than 50 feet in length and 38 feet
in breadth." Costing $18,600 at its completion in 1855, the church
was built following Putnam's instructions. The bricks used in the
sanctuary were fired especially to be used in its construction. The
Greek Revival façade features six massive pilasters supporting a heavy
entablature and pediment. Atop the bell tower was once a clock
tower that served to notify the residents of the lower part of Saratoga
Springs of the time of day. The clock tower was removed in 1933.

❾ 365 BROADWAY
Adelphi Hotel
1877 Italianate with High Victorian Gothic porch
The Adelphi was built in 1877 during Saratoga Springs' post-Civil
War building boom by William McCaffrey, a former conductor on
the Rensselaer and Saratoga Railroad. John Morrissey, one-time world
heavyweight champion, congressman, and the founder of the Saratoga
Race Course and several casinos, including one in Congress Park, was

one of the hotel's first guests. It is said that Morrissey and his friend, Commodore Cornelius Vanderbilt, frequently met at the Adelphi during racing days at the Spa. Commodore Vanderbilt was then the richest tycoon in America and a titan among titans in Saratoga. The hotel still has its grand three-story piazza, the last of its kind existing in town, from which visitors can enjoy a magnificent view of Saratoga Springs. The slender columns rising the height of the piazza lend a delicacy to the façade of the building. A medieval influence can be found in the round arched windows and in the patterns of layered brick. After standing vacant for five years, the Adelphi was carefully restored to its Victorian elegance beginning in 1978.

⑩ 437 BROADWAY
Old YMCA
c.1880 Victorian Commercial Building
Frelin Vaughan, architect
The building at 437 Broadway was built to house the city's original YMCA. It has pyramidal roofs and an atrium roof. The building originally housed shops on the main floor, a pool and a gym on the upper floors. During the 1970s, The Saratoga Associates purchased the building and restored it over time. The leaders of this architecture and planning firm were instrumental in the community efforts leading to Saratoga Springs' successful revival. The building is now used for retail stores and professional offices.

⑪ 24 CAROLINE ST.
c.1870 Italianate Commercial Building
This flatiron style-building was erected to house the grocery and dry goods business of Cornelius Fonda, whose home was also on Caroline Street near Circular Street. In the 1940s, Pepper's Cigar Shop was located here, along with a horse-betting parlor. In the city, horse

365 Broadway, Adelphi Hotel

456-470 Broadway, Ainsworth Building

rooms, somewhat like off-track betting parlors today, were open year-round with longer hours during the August race meet. Since the 1950s, this building has been occupied by Boyce and Drake, a plumbing company. The building has a unique wedge shape with a rounded corner that makes it blend into the intersection of Caroline Street and Putnam Street. Of special note are the bowed windows on the curved portion of the building.

⑫ 456-470 BROADWAY

Ainsworth Building
1871 Italianate Commercial Building
Gilbert B. Croff, architect
Seymour Ainsworth, a leader in the community, built this commercial block with shops on the first floor and offices and apartments on the upper floors. The building echoes the Canfield Casino in its style, with a bracketed cornice and round-arched windows. Its pattern is related to that of the Town Hall across Lake Avenue, achieving a stunning architectural effect on the street. The northernmost storefront, Menges and Curtis Pharmacy, is the last of the original pharmacies in the city and one of the oldest businesses. It is also a rare example of a typical 19th century storefront.

⑬ 473 BROADWAY

Adirondack Trust Company
1916 Beaux-Arts
Alfred Hopkins, architect
This impressive building was built to house the Adirondack Trust Company in 1916. The architect, Alfred Hopkins of New York City, was selected from among nine architects who submitted plans for the building. He took pains to design every aspect of the structure, including the doors, chandeliers, desks, tables and the bronze screen that incorporates symbols of the Adirondack Mountains and replicas of old Greek and Roman coins. The striking white marble façade of marble columns, cornice and frieze, symbolizes the company's prominence in the community. The crowning shield contains symbols of the region and American ideals — a stag's head, horns

473 Broadway, Adirondack Trust Company

45 Washington St., First Baptist Church

of plenty and American eagles. Magnificent bronze doors, on which scenes from life in the Adirondacks have been modeled, mark the entrance. Inside the virtues of honesty, industry and thrift are inscribed in the marble around the top of the bank's main room.

⑭ 474 BROADWAY
Saratoga Springs City Hall, The Music Hall
1871 High Victorian Italianate
Cummings and Burt, architects
Built in 1871, this is the original Town Hall, now City Hall. The architects were awarded a mere $300 for their efforts. For the first 65 years of its existence, the building was topped by a bell and clock tower used to sound the time and signal fires, calls to war and the end of war. For safety reasons, the tower was removed in 1936. The building boasts a rich array of Italianate detail including, on the Lake Avenue side, a round window reminiscent of medieval rose windows. Most of the city's municipal functions are located in the building, which houses a courtroom, office space, the city jail and, on the upper levels, a two-story theater, The Music Hall. In days past, residents could attend performances by Chauncey Olcott and Sarah Bernhardt. During the 1930s, a boxing ring replaced the performances. Today, Saratogians and visitors can still attend musical performances, public meetings and dances in the space.

⑮ 475 BROADWAY
Post Office
1910 Beaux-Arts
James Knox Taylor, architect
James Knox Taylor was the supervising architect of the United States Treasury between 1897 and 1912. During these years, he designed a number of Beaux-Arts post offices throughout the country including the one in Saratoga Springs, which announces its importance and quality through its detailing. Through the entrance, marked by massive bronze doors, is an impressive space flooded with natural light from the skylight. In 1977, the federal government decided to close the downtown post office. Then Mayor Raymond Watkin

480-494 Broadway, Collamer Building

personally sued to stop the closure and was successful. In 1993, the post office was dilapidated and was once again threatened with closure. This time it was through the efforts of Saratoga Springs' citizens that closure was avoided. They devised an approach to divide the space to incorporate a commercial tenant alongside the post office, thus creating a source of revenue with which to fund the maintenance on this historic building. Because of their creativity, Saratoga Springs citizens still have a post office on the city's main thoroughfare.

16 480-494 BROADWAY
Collamer Building
1882-1883 High Victorian Gothic
Few apartment houses existed in the mid-19th century, and those that

{ POST OFFICE MURALS }

Two murals of the Saratoga Racing Season by Guy Pene du Bois (1884-1958) grace the interior of the Saratoga Springs Post Office. Du Bois was born in New York to a family that encouraged his artistic interests. He studied with William Merritt Chase and Robert Henri. In New York, du Bois worked as a music and art critic. In 1924, he left for Paris where du Bois developed his own style of social realism. By the 1920s, du Bois' work focused primarily on scenes from fashionable life: opera-goers, bon vivants, the smart set. His works, which often contain not-so-subtle commentary, can be found in the collections of most major museums including the Whitney Museum in New York City and the Art Institute of Chicago, and are also in private collections.

Saratoga's post office murals were created under the Treasury Relief Art Project (TRAP) which supported artists from July 1935 until June 1938. Under this program, the federal government awarded commissions to fine artists to create works of art to enhance and decorate federal buildings; over 1,100 murals and sculptures around the country were created through TRAP. In 2004, the U.S. Postal Service undertook a conservation project to restore the Saratoga murals, preserving them for the next generation.

495 - 497 Broadway, Saratoga Arms

did were, for the most part, occupied by poor families. However, by the late 19th century luxury apartment buildings were all the rage in American cities. Warren B. Collamer, then a resident of neighboring Greenfield, was the first person to build a modern apartment building with retail storefronts in Saratoga Springs. The Collamer Building is a rich High Victorian composition in brick that combines Romanesque, Gothic and Queen Anne motifs. The round arches of the windows and the fancy brick work continue the pattern of detailing found in the Town Hall and make this side of the street a complete composition. Today, the building is used for offices on the upper floors and retail space on the street level.

⑰ 487 BROADWAY

1885, Richardsonian Romanesque
R. Newton Brezee, architect
This building was built for Davis Coleman, a cigar manufacturer whose business was located at 382 Broadway. Mr. Coleman lived in the upper stories of the building until his death in 1896. On the ground floor, the tenants were Eddy & Ryan, a bakery and dairy kitchen. The influence of architect Henry Hobson Richardson can be seen in the checkerboard detail, the terra cotta rosettes and other medieval ornament, and in the heavy rounded arches.

⑱ 495 BROADWAY

Saratoga Arms
1870 Second Empire
Lewis E. Whiting built 491 to 497 Broadway in 1870 and operated it as a boarding house until his death in 1882. The property was then divided into 491, 493 and 495-497. Dr. James Mingay, a druggist whose pharmacy was located at 470 Broadway (now Menges and Curtis), purchased 491 as his residence in 1882. Dr. Taber B. Reynolds, a physician and president of the Saratoga County Medical Society purchased 493 Broadway. And 495-497 Broadway was used by Loren B. Putnam, Gideon Putnam's grandson, for several years before it was sold to Dr. Byron Murray, a physician and surgeon. Over the years, 495 Broadway has been operated as a rooming house under several names including The Putnam, The Walton and The Windsor. The building was restored in 1998 and opened as a hotel.

505-509 Broadway

⑲ 41 LONG ALLEY
c.1870 Carriage House

This building is believed to have been the carriage house to 491 Broadway, built when Dr. Mingay owned the house. When carriages were replaced by automobiles, the building became a garage, then later an art gallery. It was renovated in 1979 to house an architectural firm. Alleys, similar to Long Alley, can be found throughout the city's neighborhoods. Built originally as places where horses and carriages could be housed and from which servants could enter the main houses, the alleys often became housing for the working class. Today the vernacular buildings and barns along the alleys have mostly been restored and adapted for residences and professional offices.

⑳ 505 BROADWAY
c.1834 Greek Revival

Judge Nicholas B. Doe built this house in 1841. Judge Doe's name was associated with Saratoga County politics from its earliest days. He was elected a member of the state Assembly in 1825 and again in 1840 and served as a county judge. In 1866, Paoli Durkee purchased the house. Durkee was one of the early schoolmasters in Saratoga Springs, setting up the first classical school for boys. His son, Cornelius, is best remembered as an early Saratoga Springs historian, whose book *Reminiscences of Saratoga* recounts the people and sights of Saratoga Springs in the 1800s. The building is a fine, intact example of a Greek Revival city house. Its endwalls rise to the parapets with chimneys. Across the front is a lovely original entablature. The 12-paned windows with their simple brownstone lintels are original. Today, the building is used as offices for a real estate firm.

㉑ 509 BROADWAY
Temple Sinai
c.1890 Colonial Revival

This was originally the site of the home of John M. Davison, a printer, and his family. Mr. Davison was also the president and superintendent of the Saratoga and Whitehall Railroad. He died in 1890 and the house was sold to Dr. Frederick J. Ressiguie, who either vastly remodeled the house or constructed a new one, which cannot be determined with certainty. Dr. Ressigue died in 1956

487 Broadway

leaving the house to the YMCA. The building has many beautiful colonial details including the ground-floor bay windows, the Adamesque garlands, a pseudo- Federal porch at the entrance and a beautiful upper-story colonnade with windows. In 1974, the house was acquired by the Temple Sinai and is today home to a vibrant congregation.

㉒ 504-520 BROADWAY
Algonquin
1892-1893 Richardsonian Romanesque
S. Gifford Slocum, architect
One of the most important buildings in Saratoga Springs, the Algonquin was the second luxury residential apartment building with fine shops on the lower level built on Broadway. The building takes its name from the Algonquin Indian nation, the study of which was a hobby of James H. Pardue, the owner and builder. The Algonquin is one of the most elaborate pieces of architecture in Saratoga Springs. Notice the asymmetrical façade and bricks laid in geometric patterns. The variety of porches, arcades supported by columns, and arches bring a lively rhythm to the building. A checkerboard pattern appears in panels on the façade. The integration of all these elements creates an aggressive three-dimensionality reminiscent of the work of architect Henry Hobson Richardson.

㉓ 511 BROADWAY
Moriarta House
c. 1885 Richardson Romanesque
R. Newton Brezee, architect
This house was built for Dr. Douglas C. Moriarta, a prominent physician, surgeon and medical pioneer who used radium and insulin to treat his patients. A member of a leading Saratoga family, Dr. Moriarta was the brother of Webster C. Moriarta, who was president of the Vichy Spring Company for 35 years. The house is a fine example of a mixed Queen Anne and Richardson Romanesque design. Of particular note is the exceptional detailing with rock-faced masonry bordering arches of varying scale. The round tower in the corner sports a candlesnuffer cap often found in Saratoga Springs architecture. The fantastic Queen Anne style gable in the roof has a typical depressed Queen Anne window. Just north of the Moriarta

House, is a small wooden cottage built in the 1830s that once housed the gardener who cared for Dr. Moriarta's garden.

㉔ 517 BROADWAY
Community Theater
1937 Colonial Revival

Reade's Community Theater opened its doors on July 28, 1937, with a showing of *Lost Horizon*, with seating for 1,200 people. On its 20th anniversary, an article in *The Saratogian* newspaper described the building as "a startling departure in the theater architecture for those accustomed to the blazing marquees and rococo decoration of older theaters." Marked by colossal white columns and a red brick façade trimmed in limestone, this Colonial Revival theater was truly a departure from the traditional. According to *The Saratogian*, world-famous theater architect Thomas Lamb developed this unique

{ DOWNTOWN MOVIE HOUSES }

It is believed that the first movie was shown in Saratoga Springs in 1897 — just three years after Thomas Edison invented his movie machine. Thomas Costello opened the first movie theater, Dreamland, in a small one-story building on the corner of West Congress and Broadway where the Visitor Center is today. Soon a second theater, the Edisonia, opened nearby and could seat 250 people. Both of these theaters closed soon after opening. In 1907, the Bijou opened at 486 Broadway in the Collamer Building. The success of the Bijou encouraged other businessman to open movie houses; soon movie theaters and vaudeville theaters could be found up and down Broadway.

In 1919, The Congress Theater opened at 322 Broadway. Its owner was Senator Edgar T. Brackett. His son, Charles Brackett, and Billy Wilder produced and directed such the Oscar winning films as *The Lost Weekend*(1945), *Sunset Boulevard* (1950), and the original *Titanic* (1953). Senator Brackett had the ballroom of the Congress Hall Hotel converted into a theater that featured wide marble stairs, ornamental railings, plush blue carpeting and a blue velvet curtain spanning a stage 50 feet wide by 27 feet deep. Oscar Hammerstein produced and starred in the musical "Somebody's Sweetheart" for the opening of the theater. The first film was presented at The Congress two nights later — *Daddy Long Legs*, starring Mary Pickford. The Congress Theater closed in 1960. After many years without a downtown movie theater, Saratogians can once again go to the movies on Broadway. The Saratoga Film Forum, a non-profit organization, screens independent and foreign films weekly at the Saratoga County Arts Council at 320 Broadway.

Source: Poor Richards Almanac, September 1996

design for mogul Walter Reade, who owned a large chain of theaters. Reade liked the design so much he built one in Saratoga Springs and another in Hudson, New York. Competition from mall theaters eventually meant the end of the Community Theater and it closed in 1978 leaving the historic downtown without a cinema. Renovated and adapted for use as a real estate office in 2000, its original ticket booth can still be found in front of the building.

㉕ 543 BROADWAY
Old Firehouse
1884 Romanesque Revival
S. Gifford Slocum, architect
This building, with its two heavy, rock-framed arches, was designed by S. Gifford Slocum. It served as the city's firehouse until the new building opened on Lake Avenue in 1930. It is now used as a retail store and restaurant. Artifacts from the original firehouse are on view at the Saratoga History Museum in the Canfield Casino.

㉖ 123 MAPLE AVE.
Bryan House
1826 Federal Style
The Bryan House sits on the oldest inhabited site in Saratoga Springs. The original inn was a crude log cabin built in 1773 by Dirck Schoughten of Waterford. In 1774, John Arnold and his family took over the cabin, improved it and operated an inn for visitors to the High Rock Spring. In 1777, the inn was purchased by the Norton family who operated it successfully for 10 years. Alexander Bryan purchased the inn in 1787 to operate it in his retirement. Bryan was a Revolutionary War hero who spied on the British troops near Fort Edward, ultimately aiding in their defeat in the Battle of Saratoga. Bryan's crude inn was the only accomodations in Saratoga Springs until Gideon Putnam constructed the Union Hall in 1803. In 1826, John Bryan built the stone house on the site of his father's tavern. The house was converted into a restaurant beginning in 1979. Many of the original architectural elements remain, particularly the 12-over-12 windows and the oval windows under the gable ends.

1517 Broadway Community Theater Building

FRANKLIN

SQUARE

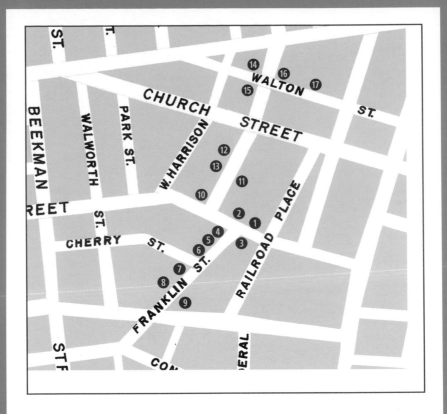

TOUR DETAILS

Distance: 1 mile

Steps: 1,823

Time: Approximately 25 minutes

Terrain: Some steady, gradual inclines, one hill

Directions: Start at Division St. and Railroad Place. Franklin Square to Franklin St., south on Franklin St. to Washington St., reverse and north on Franklin St. to Franklin Square. Square to Clinton St., north on Clinton St., cross Church St., to Walton St. Walton St. east to Woodlawn Ave., Woodlawn Ave. south to Division St., then west to Franklin Square.

TOUR HIGHLIGHTS

- ❶ 1 Franklin Square
- ❷ 3 Franklin Square
- ❸ 2 Franklin Square
- ❹ 4 Franklin Square
- ❺ 59 Franklin St.
- ❻ 63 Franklin St.
- ❼ 47 Franklin St.
- ❽ 39 Franklin St.
- ❾ 36 Franklin St.
- ❿ 6 Franklin Square
- ⓫ 22 Clinton Street
- ⓬ 1 –5 Clinton Place
- ⓭ 13-25 Thomas St.
- ⓮ 75 Clinton St.
- ⓯ 72 Walton St.
- ⓰ 76 Clinton St.
- ⓱ 45 Walton St.

*F*ranklin Square is located just two blocks west of Broadway on Division Street. When the Square was developed in the 1820s and 1830s, it stood on the edge of town, a buffer between the surrounding woodlands and Broadway's urban environment.

During the 1830s and 1840s, Franklin Square became the fashionable place for homes of some of the community's leading families, who built their houses to look like temples in the Greek Revival style honoring the Greeks as models of republican virtue.

By the 1860s, the character of Franklin Square had changed; it was no longer primarily residential. A number of hotels and cure institutes had popped up around the Square. These cure institutes, which were founded by doctors of hydrotherapy, had many of America's famous and stylish flocking to the springs to heal their ailments and ease the stress of cosmopolitan society. As the city became an increasingly popular vacation destination, Franklin Square grew. In the 1880s, the hotels and lodges of Franklin Square flourished, their architecture was experimental and flamboyant. A fountain bubbling Saratoga Springs' wondrous water was erected in the Square, symbolic of the quality of life in the neighborhood.

But in the years following the Civil War, wealthy residents turned their focus north toward North Broadway, and Franklin Square became less and less of a focal point. Many of its properties fell into disrepair.

In 1967, a headline in *The Saratogian* newspaper read "Todd House Faces Demolition." New York State had proposed an east-west arterial running through the west side of Saratoga Springs. In addition to demolishing the Todd House in Franklin Square along with about 35 other houses, the arterial as it was proposed would have effectively cut off the downtown commercial district. A grassroots group called the Citizen's Organization for Progress in Saratoga Springs formed to oppose this project. Largely because of their advocacy efforts, the project was defeated.

2 Franklin Square, Adirondack Lodge

During the 1980s, Franklin Square began to experience a renaissance. Individuals who had understood the significance of the Square saw the potential in this magnificent old neighborhood and began rehabilitating the homes and buildings.

❶ 1 FRANKLIN SQUARE
Augustus Bockes House
1834 Greek Revival
The yellow limestone house with a magnificent columned portico in the central section, balanced on either side by rectangular colonnaded wings, was built during the 1830s. It was the home of Augustus Bockes, a well-known Saratoga Springs lawyer who later became a state judge. In about 1875, Bockes moved to a new house at 30 Circular St.

❷ 3 FRANKLIN SQUARE
James Marvin House
1836 Greek Revival
This house was the home of James Marvin, one of Saratoga Springs' most successful businessmen. With his brother, Thomas, (whose house was also in the Square at No. 4) he established the Bank of Saratoga Springs. He was also a director of the Saratoga and Schenectady Railroad, the railway that ferried visitors to the city. Marvin had a successful political career which took him to Washington D.C., where he served three terms in the House of Representatives. This Greek Revival house is notable for its square pillars, assymetrical doorway, and full-story windows on the first floor. An upstairs porch, which was most likely added in the late 19th or early 20th century, cuts through the original two-story Greek Revival porch.

❸ 2 FRANKLIN SQUARE
Adirondack Lodge
c.1870 French Renaissance
The first owner of this house was George Harvey whose lumber

business, Harvey & Co., was located nearby on Division and Walworth streets near the Adirondack Railroad track. This flamboyant building reflects the spirited nature of Saratoga Springs in the post-Civil War era. The gallery and veranda-like porches are brought together by horizontal belt courses and moldings in the classical style and are reminiscent of a southern plantation. As the years passed, the house changed greatly with a grand addition to the south, most likely in 1900-1901, for a medical institute. The addition was so large that it encroached on the house at 66 Franklin St.. George Crippen, one of the proprietors of Crippen & Reid, manufacturers of ladies wrappers and house dresses, owned 66 Franklin, and was forced to move out of the Square and built 55 Union Ave. that same year. From 1894 to 1918, Sara McEwen, widow of Dr. Robert McEwen, operated a boardinghouse here, which she named the Adirondack Lodge. After years of neglect, the building was restored in the 1980s and is now used as offices and apartments.

❹ 4 FRANKLIN SQUARE
Marvin-Sackett-Todd House
1832 Greek Revival

The house at 4 Franklin Square was home to a number of influential and important Saratogians. Thomas Marvin built this house during the 1830s. He and his brother, James, were community leaders during the antebellum era. Thomas Marvin was an attorney, judge and member of the state Assembly. He served as the community postmaster during the administrations of both President Tyler and President Polk and is known for having secured the first charter in the state for the first mutual fire insurance company. Following Marvin's death, the Sackett family occupied the house. William Sackett had been a member of Congress from 1848 to 1853, where he was a leader in the fight against slavery. At the close of his congressional

3 Franklin Square

14 Franklin Square

term, Sackett moved to Saratoga Springs, where he married Mary Marvin, daughter of Thomas Marvin.

In 1926, following the death of Mary Marvin Sackett, the Todd family became owners of the property. Hiram C. Todd practiced law in Saratoga Springs as a partner in the same law firm as Senator Edgar Brackett. He left his firm in Saratoga Springs to join the New York City law firm of Baldwin, Todd and Lefferts — incidentally, Richard M. Nixon was also a partner in this firm. Todd is perhaps best known as a special prosecutor who was a key figure during the Tammany Hall corruption hearings. In 1930, New York Governor Herbert Lehman appointed Todd to handle the Samuel Druckman slaying prosecution.

The temple front and recessed door are examples of the Greek Revival style, while the massive rectangular block frame, upper balustrade and cupola belong to the Georgian tradition. The polygonal bays were added in the 1850s. The Victorian door was added in the 1870s. Originally, the house was ornamented with wrought iron balconies; these were removed in the 20th century.

❺ 59 FRANKLIN ST.

Stover House
c.1830 Greek Revival
With many visitors seeking cures from the natural springs of Saratoga Springs, the opening of the Saratoga and Schenectady Railroad in 1832 brought more people, wealth and an influx of ideas and trends to the city. The Greek Revival house at 59 Franklin St. represents this period of wealth and prosperity prior to the Civil War. It and the house at 63 Franklin are two of the best examples of vernacular Greek Revival style in Saratoga Springs. The earliest known owner of 59 Franklin St. was Rev. Ensign Stover, pastor of the Methodist Episcopal Church. From 1890 to 1927, the house was the home of the Waterbury family. Herman Waterbury married Rev. Stover's daughter, Louisa, and was the manager of the local Western Union office. The house's first floor has lovely, tall, multi-paned windows and surrounding a six-panel door is a full transom light and full-length sidelights. Also noteworthy is the dentil trim on the cornice. This trim is repeated in the inside of the gable front pediment.

❻ 63 FRANKLIN ST.

Bennett House
c. 1830 Greek Revival
This house is very similar to the adjacent house at 59 Franklin St. Built in the Greek Revival style, this was the home of William Bennett, proprietor of the American Hotel, one of the city's few year-round hotels, located on Broadway south of the United States Hotel.

6 Franklin Square   59 Franklin St.

⑦ 47 FRANKLIN ST.

Harnessmaker's Home

c.1820 Federal

This house is one of the oldest houses in the city, dating from the 1820s. When it was built, this house would have stood near the edge of town and may have been a farmhouse. In the years following its original construction, an addition to the front of the house was probably done, reflecting perhaps the growing prosperity of the owners and neighborhood. The façade of the house, which features a demarcated entablature with its panels and windows, is Greek Revival in design. Notice the eyebrow windows located in the frieze. By the mid-19th century, the house belonged to Theodore Coller, who, according to the Saratoga Springs city directory, owned a bowling saloon on South Broadway near the railroad tracks.

⑧ 39 FRANKLIN ST.

Morey House

c.1850 Greek Revival

The house was the home of Nathan Morey, owner of a meat market. During the 1870s, Nathan and his brother, Robert, formed one of Saratoga Springs' earliest baseball clubs. Among the house's Greek Revival details are brownstone lintels and an entablature window. The cornice picks up the emerging Italianate style. Significant renovations in the early 20th century added large Colonial Revival style windows to the façade.

⑨ 36 FRANKLIN ST.

c. 1815 Federal

The oldest surviving house in the city, this Federal style residence originally had chimneys at each end. Original rolled-glass windows have been relocated to the rear of the house. During an 1845 remodeling, carpenter Gothic details were added along with the front gable. The date of this remodeling was discovered in the 1980s when the owner found newspapers dating from 1845 packed into the window frames. The front porch was added in the 1870s.

75 Clinton St.

72 Walton St.

{ SARATOGA HOSPITAL
FOUNDERS AND MANAGERS }

In the late 1880s, a young woman was shot on a street in Saratoga Springs. She was taken to the only public medical facility in the city, a room in the police station at the Saratoga Springs Town Hall. The young woman died of her injuries, an outcome almost predictable given the makeshift surroundings. This incident, and others like it, spurred a group of intelligent, accomplished and compassionate women to establish a true hospital in Saratoga Springs, the first community hospital in the country founded and managed entirely by women. It was not unusual for women in the latter half of the 19th century to involve themselves in health-related causes. Women were enlisted by the Civil War Sanitary Commissions to provide medial supplies. Committees of visiting women could be found in hospitals providing assistance and comfort to patients. But outside of maternity and pediatric hospitals, women were rarely found in leadership roles.

Beginning in 1891, over the course of three and a half years, the women planned for and raised the money to start the hospital. They found the perfect building in 1893, purchased it for $6,000 and spent the next two years upgrading it with gas lighting, a system of bells and annunciators on each floor and steam heat. When they were finished, the new hospital had space for 15 beds, including 12 for adults and three for children. There were equal numbers of beds for men and women. And there were five private rooms and an operating room. The doors to the Saratoga Hospital, located in a substantial three-story Second Empire house just west of Franklin Square at the corner of West Harrison and Division streets, opened on July 25, 1895.

The women whose purposeful dedication to providing quality medical care to one and all built Saratoga Hospital were: Rosanna Andrews, Lillian J.E.W. Bockes, Kate M. Crippen, Margaret C. Foley, Jennie A. Grenning, Aimee L. Hanson, Caroline W. Lawrence, Katherine D.B. McKnight, Margaret Minick, Frances E. Putnam, Helen B. Rich, Minerva L. Rickard, Susan P. Ritchie, and Anna R. Strong - 14 women whose names we know because they insisted that, counter to convention, each sign the documents forming the hospital with both her first and last names.

1-5 Clinton Place

⑩ 6 FRANKLIN SQUARE
Hotel Carlsbad
1840
While the hotel dates from 1840, this building was extensively renovated in the 1870s and 1890s, altering its appearance and character greatly. The gambrel roof at the front of the building is reflective of the Colonial Revival style and was added during these renovations. In 1899, the Hotel Carlsbad opened its doors to the public. Owned by Dr. E. Valencourt Duell, who was also the hotel's physician, the hotel was known for its gourmet cuisine and spa-type treatments. In 1919, the property became known as the Hotel Russell. The restoration of this building in 1982, after standing vacant for 13 years, marks the beginning of the renaissance of Franklin Square.

⑪ 22 CLINTON ST.
A.P. Edwards House
c. 1850 Greek Revival
Constructed around the 1850, this house typifies the conclusion of the Greek Revival era. Its stone lintels and expansive frieze with eyebrow openings date it around the middle of the 19th century. The earliest owner of this home was A.F. Edwards, a civil engineer. This house is more commonly associated with a later owner, Sam Sague, a businessman who ran a lumber, grain, wine, coal and wood business on commercially-oriented Church Street. The windows and porch are Victorian additions from Sague's time. Throughout its history, the building has been occupied by many Saratoga Springs merchants. In the mid-to late-1900s, the building was part of the G.F. Blackmer Company, a paper and office supply business whose main building was located just to the north. An interesting feature of this house is the observatory in the center of the roof.

⑫ 1 –5 CLINTON PLACE
Clinton Place Row
c.1872 Second Empire Row House
Built slightly before 1872 by Walter J. Hendrick, this block of

attached houses reflects the city's increasing urbanization. Of note are the slight variations in the rhythm of the roofline with the first, third and fifth having similar detail. Some of the original iron roof cresting survives on 1 Clinton Place. These rowhouses are an enduring example of the diversity of Franklin Square's residents. At one time, the houses were home to the pastor of the Methodist Episcopal Church, the owner of the boot and shoe shop, an attorney, a physician, and a surgeon. One of the most noted tenants of Clinton Place was Charles Paul, editor and proprietor of *The Saratogian* newspaper. Another well-known resident was George Gillis, bookkeeper of the United States Hotel. The Saratoga Springs Preservation Foundation restored the house at 5 Clinton Place.

⑬ 13-25 THOMAS ST.

1876 High Victorian
Frelin Vaughan, architect
Walter J. Hendrick built the seven row houses on Thomas Street in 1876 on land adjacent to his coal and lumber yard. The business, known as Hendrick's Coal and Lumber, also included a grocery store. The 1884 insurance maps list the seven houses as tenements; residents included laborers in the building trades, and on the railroads. Each wood-framed row house has three window bays and a covered entrance.

⑭ 75 CLINTON ST.

Henry Hanson House
1866 High Victorian Gothic
This house, the home of Henry Hanson, was built at the end of the Civil War. Hanson was the vice president and director of the First National Bank, and owned a prosperous business on the corner of Church and Clinton streets, selling groceries, feed, grain, liquor, coal, wood and lumber. Living here allowed Hanson to maintain a hands-on approach to business. The houses on the four corners of the intersection of Clinton and Walton represent the dominant architectural styles in Saratoga Springs before and after the Civil War. The house at 75 Clinton, which, along with the houses at 720 and 722 North Broadway, was used as a setting for the movie *Ghost Story*, has dramatic architectural details. A cantilevered two-story bay over a Romanesque arched entrance is one of the dominant features of the building. On the north side, a semi-hexagonal bay runs the full height of the building.

⑮ 72 WALTON ST.

c.1878 Second Empire
The house at 72 Walton was built for Samuel H. Luther, a liquor agent who lived there with his wife, Rhoda, until his death. She

remained in the house until 1901, when the house was sold to
Charles E. Van Pelt, manager of Armour & Company, a wholesale
beef warehouse that was located on the southwest corner of Church
Street and Railroad Place. During this time, the house was used as
a two-family residence, although there is no evidence of a second
kitchen. Charles Van Pelt died on Jan. 5,1917, exactly 25 years to the
day after Samuel Luther. Among the notable architectural details is a
lovely three-story protruding bay window, a stained-glass window in
an upstairs bath, and dormer windows with turned poles and caps.

⑯ 76 CLINTON ST.

1894 Colonial Revival

This house was built for Stephen Richards, a successful businessman
who specialized in the sale of coal, lumber, groceries, grain, kerosene
oil, and wines – all commodities necessary to satisfy the demands
of a thriving city. The house has a wonderful variety of window
styles, including the Georgian style fan lights, and the Medieval style
stained glass. The gambrel roof and the variety of surface textures and
window shapes are typical of the Colonial Revival style in this region.

⑰ 45 WALTON ST.

1841 Greek Revival

The townhouse at 45 Walton St. was built as the home of Samuel
Fisher, a carriage and sleigh maker. It sits on a high stone rubble
foundation, with large windows to light the cellar. The façade is
granite and brownstone, probably transported up the Hudson River.
On the east side of the house is a small porch that is designed as a
miniature temple with columns and an entablature, but no pediment.

76 Clinton St.

145 Walton St.

DUBLIN

DUBLIN

DRAWN BY HOTEL & RAILROAD
WORK, IRISH & THEN ITALIAN
IMMIGRANTS POPULATED THIS
SPECIAL NEIGHBORHOOD FROM
THE 1840s THROUGH THE 1890s.

CITY OF SARATOGA SPRINGS 1999

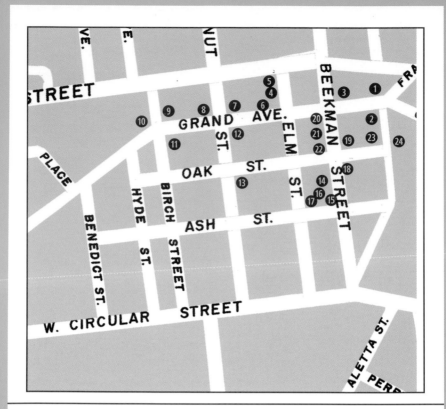

TOUR DETAILS

Distance: 0.87 miles

Steps: 1,750

Time: Approximately 20 minutes

Terrain: Flat, very uneven sidewalks. Some street signs missing at Elm and Oak streets

Directions: Note: this tour takes you down and back several side streets. Start at 117 Grand Ave. West on Grand Ave. to Elm St., north on Elm St. to Washington St. Reverse, south on Elm St. to Grand Ave. West on Grand Ave to Birch St. Reverse and east on Grand Ave. to Elm St. South on Elm St. to Oak St. East on Oak St. to Beekman St. South on Beekman St. to Ash St. West on Ash St. one block. Reverse, east on Ash St. to Beekman St. North on Beekman St. to Grand Ave. Reverse, south on Beekman St. to Oak St. East on Oak St. to S. Franklin St. North on S. Franklin St. to Grand Ave.

TOUR HIGHLIGHTS

❶ 117 Grand Ave.
❷ 120 Grand Ave.
❸ 139 Grand Ave.
❹ 215 Elm St.
❺ 217-219 Elm St.
❻ 167 Grand Ave.
❼ 187 Grand Ave.
❽ 197 Grand Ave.
❾ 215 Grand Ave
❿ 225 Grand Ave.
⓫ 220 Grand Ave.
⓬ 190-194 Grand Ave.
⓭ 42 Oak St.
⓮ 55 Beekman St.
⓯ 47 Ash St.
⓰ 51 Ash St.
⓱ 61 Ash St.
⓲ 68 Beekman St.
⓳ 70 Beekman St.
⓴ 79 Beekman St.
㉑ 73 Beekman St.
㉒ 69 Beekman St.
㉓ 13 Oak St.
㉔ So. Franklin at Oak Street

140

The West Side neighborhood of Saratoga Springs is often referred to as "Dublin," reflecting its roots as an ethnic neighborhood. This lovely neighborhood, with its modest homes and small businesses, was developed in the 1830s largely by Irish immigrants who provided labor for the booming building industry and in the hotels. In the years before the Irish immigrants settled in Dublin, African-Americans who worked for the hotels and railroads lived in homes along Congress Street. Unfortunately, few of these houses remain to remind us of the early history of the West Side.

By 1880, Italian immigrants were making their way to Saratoga Springs to work on railroad construction as well as important city landmarks. Bringing skills from the Old World, they often became bricklayers, masons or stonecutters. Like other newcomers, the Italian immigrants commonly settled on Saratoga Springs' West Side, moving into houses vacated by earlier immigrant families that had prospered and settled in other parts of the city. The new Italian residents eventually opened grocery stores, shoemaker shops, barber shops and several restaurants within blocks of each other, creating a sort of "Little Italy" on the West Side. Elegant homes were built on the West Side's upper Grand Avenue and Washington Street in the 1860s and 1870s as West Side workers and merchants prospered with the success of Saratoga Springs.

Evidence of the skills and trades brought by these ethnic groups still remains in the architecture and landscaping of Dublin. The carpenters who lived in the West Side added extra architectural motifs to otherwise unpretentious vernacular structures. The Irish carpenters had built classic Greek Revival houses with formal fronts and white picket fences; these fences would be replaced with the craftsmanship of the stone masons from Italy. The Italian masons practiced their skills in their own neighborhood creating unique designs and raising the quality of a 19th century working-class neighborhood.

Along with the Irish and the Italians, African-Americans played an important role in the development of the West Side. In the late 1800s

117 Grand Ave.

120 Grand Ave.

and early 1900s, a new generation of African-American residents settled on the West Side to be close to the big hotels where many were employed. Soon, African-American owned businesses began to prosper in the neighborhood. Jazz clubs, bars and restaurants created a pulsating nightlife on Congress Street and Grand Avenue.

In the 1960s and 1970s, the urban renewal movement razed the buildings where these businesses had flourished and for several decades the neighborhood languished. Today, however, the area is home to an arts district, filled with galleries and studios. The neighborhood offers visitors a view of a Saratoga Springs working-class neighborhood that has retained its unique ethnic influences. The 19th century herringbone patterned brick walks, two-tier porches, and stone work created by the skills of the Italian masons still can be found. The railroad tracks and most of the hotels are gone now, but the homes and buildings that were built by those who built the railroad have remained.

Sources:
James Kettlewell, "Everything You Ever Wanted to Know about Saratoga Springs," Saratoga Beat, Summer 2001.
University at Albany Planning Studio, "Planning and Design Recommendations for the West Side Neighborhood, Saratoga Springs, NY,"

❶ 117 GRAND AVE.

c. 1884 Queen Anne

This unusual building was originally the headquarters and depot for the Adirondack Railroad Company, a railroad that transported mined iron ore from the Adirondack Mountains. The first locomotive to arrive at the new depot was named the General Hancock, after a general who was killed in the Battle of Gettysburg. The railroad operated from this site until 1902, when it went bankrupt. The Delaware and Hudson took over the line and the federal government subsequently added an additional 20 miles of track to haul lead mined to make ammunition during World War II. After the line was abandoned in the 1960s, a former employee of the railroad took up residence in the house. He later rented the house to the Tillman family who raised their 12 children here.

Of particular interest in the building are the large arched picture

215 Grand Ave.

windows on the front and side of the building, and the heavy rock-faced stone foundation capped with massive timbers. Notice also the Victorian Gothic details in the steeply pitched roof and the decorative chimney pot. The building was purchased by the Saratoga Springs Preservation Foundation in the 1990s. Nearing ruin, the building was renovated and reconfigured to meet the needs of low-income renters and commercial tenants.

❷ 120 GRAND AVE.
c.1870 Italianate

The house at 120 Grand Ave., first owned by artist David Pierce, was located in the center of the hustle and bustle of the West Side. Across the street, markets flourished and the railroad tracks passed directly next to the house. For much of the life of the house, it was the home of the Figelman family, owners of a scrap business located behind the house. After many years of standing empty, the house was purchased by private owners and extensively restored. The gable with the circular window is a classic symbol of the Italianate style. The beautiful High Victorian window treatment is an outstanding element of the design of the house. Also worth noting are the broad front porch and the carved wooden double doors.

❸ 139 GRAND AVE.
c. 1854 Greek Revival

Artemus Barrett and his wife, Fidelia, built this house in 1854. Mr. Barrett, a hatter and owner of a men's accessories business on Broadway, was a prominent member of the Saratoga Springs business scene and lived here until his death at the age of 89. This is a fine example of the aesthetic quality of small Greek Revival houses.

❹ 215 ELM ST.
c. 1850 Greek Revival

Blackmer & Son, a paper goods business, was established at this location in 1868. It grew, prospered and relocated, in 1885, to a larger building at 157 Washington St., and in 1918, to an even larger building on Clinton Street. This building has elements of the Greek Revival style with a low-pitched roof and cornice. The early Victorian brackets were probably added in the 1860s. It is larger in size and scale than the surrounding structures, probably due to its origin as a

215 Elm St.

commercial building. The entrance is at the street level, with a spiral staircase to the second story. The building is now a single-family residence.

⑤ 217-219 ELM ST.
c. 1870 Vernacular, 2 family residence
Charles Dobbins, a bookkeeper, and his wife, Fannie, a clerk, were the first owners of this building. Meeting the need for housing affordable for working families is a challenge in many successful communities, none more so than in Saratoga Springs. This double house is typical of the affordable housing built for workers in the late 19th century. A straightforward design, the architectural detailing of this modest house makes it a lovely addition to the neighborhood. Of particular notice is the false front-curved cornice, the central two-story projecting bay and the small entry porch for each entrance.

⑥ 167 GRAND AVE.
c. 1887
R. Newton Brezee, architect
Brezee designed this house for A.P. Knapp, a butcher who operated Waring & Knapp at 116 Congress St.. In 1895, Knapp opened Delmonico's Market at 432 Broadway. The design of this building is simple and sparely ornamented. Of particular note is the two-story polygonal bay that continues into the front pedimented gable and the twinned-chamfered porch posts.

⑦ 187 GRAND AVE.
c. 1868 Italianate
In this impressive house we see the work of the skilled immigrant craftsmen who settled on the West Side. The design of this house is perhaps one of the finest in Saratoga Springs. In 1868, the city directory lists Buel Thresher, a carpenter, at 187 Grand Ave. Mr. Thresher lived here until 1880, when it became the home of Benjamin Goldsmith, a grocer. Of particular note is the wooden sheathing cut and patterned to resemble stone, and the quoins that have been similarly constructed. The open porch that runs the width

of the house is fashioned with chamfered posts. The projecting center bay that extends from the second story to the third story with triple High Victorian Gothic windows was added in the 1880s. In front of the house, you will find original wrought-iron fencing.

⑧ 197 GRAND AVE.
c. 1870 Second Empire
Built by Edward Noble, a wealthy New York City stockbroker who lived there until the early 1900s, this is one of the more impressive structures on upper Grand Avenue. Notice particularly its mansard roof with patterned slates.

⑨ 215 GRAND AVE.
c. 1888 Queen Anne
The house at 215 Grand is typical of late 19th century vernacular residential architecture, combined with Queen Anne style elements, such as a variety of textures in its siding and wrap around porches. Of particular note are the turned porch posts with jigsaw-cut ornamentation. In 1890, the city directory lists Simon W. Barrett, carpenter, as residing at 215 Grand Ave..

⑩ 225 GRAND AVE.
c. 1855 Greek Revival
The house at 225 Grand Ave. was built in the Greek Revival style with typical elements such as narrow sidelights around the entrance door and flat lintels above the windows. The residence first appears on the 1858 map of Saratoga Springs on property owned by Rockwell Putnam, Gideon Putnam's son. The property was worked as a farm for several years. By 1900, the house was the residence of W. Alexander Ashton, an engineer with the D&H Railroad.

187 Grand Ave.

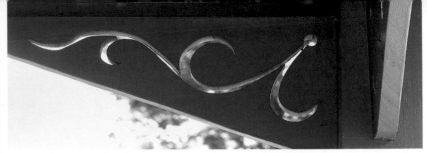

220 Grand Ave. porch detail

⑪ 220 GRAND AVE.

c. 1880 Greek Revival/Italianate

In 1883, this building was the home of John Foster of Foster &
Lohnas Blacksmiths, manufacturers of carriages and sleighs, whose
shop was located at the corner of Thomas and Lawrence streets.
Stylistically, the building combines elements of the Greek Revival and
Italianate styles. By the 1920s and 1930s, a bakery had been added
on to the building. While no longer used as a bakery, the addition is
a reminder of the neighborhood groceries and small businesses that
were prevalent throughout Dublin.

⑫ 190-194 GRAND AVE.

1896 Romanesque Revival

R. Newton Brezee, architect

Michael F. Meehan, a Saratoga Springs' police commissioner, built
these row houses as investment property. Meehan lived on the
opposite corner at 196 Grand Ave.. A dairyman, a bank bookkeeper,
and the proprietor of a furniture store originally occupied the houses.
The building provides a fine example of Brezee's work beyond the
single-family residence for which he is renowned and is a fine, but
simple, example of the Romanesque Revival style.

⑬ 42 OAK ST.

c. 1874 Victorian Vernacular

This house is believed to have been built at the end of the 19th
century as a multipurpose building. Of particular note on this
building are the High Victorian windows. Added onto the house
was a barbershop, in business until the early 1950s. Anthony and
Rose Bencivegna lived here with their seven children. The couple's
sons ran the barbershop. The home was a popular hangout for the
neighborhood. Neighbors young and old were welcome to share
good company and take part in the Bencievegna's delicacies during
the Principessa Elena Society's annual St. Michael's Festival.

⑭ 55 BEEKMAN ST.

c. 1885 Victorian Vernacular

In the early 1900s, after Italian immigrants had moved into the
neighborhood bringing new skilled craftsmen to the area, Nicholas
Sabino Sr. set up a shoe repair in the rear of this building. As the

business grew, his son remodeled the first story to accommodate the flourishing shop, which continued to operate until 2005 in the same location.

⑮ 47 ASH ST.
c. 1883 Victorian Vernacular, two-family residence
The early owners and residents of 47 Ash St. reflect the history of the Dublin neighborhood. The Saratoga Springs directory in 1883 lists James Welch, hackman, as residing here; in 1900, Nathan Whipple, engineer at the Adirondack Railroad, and Berthold Whipple, helper at the D&H roundhouse, were residents. The original features of the building are obscured by artificial siding.

⑯ 51 ASH ST.
c. 1850 Greek Revival
The design of this building is principally Greek Revival, and represents, in its details, early building practices, such as short clapboards. For many years, a grocery store was located at this corner. In 1878, William Kelly and John O'Rourke, grocers, had a store here. In 1883, John O'Rourke took over the business and added a liquor store. By 1890, O'Rourke had sold his business to John A'Hearn.

{ MARIANNA FERRARA}

Marianna Ferrera and her 1-year-old son made the journey across the Atlantic to join Domenico Ferrera who had immigrated from Italy a year earlier, in 1887. A midwife, Mary Ann assisted in the delivery of hundreds of babies over the next 60 years. Even today, many West Side residents recall seeing Mary Ann outfitted with her black bag on her way to the bedside of a soon-to-be mother. Mary Ann was first licensed to practice midwifery in 1915 by the New York State Department of Health. She had a special touch with difficult births. A small woman with delicate hands, Mary Ann was often able to turn a baby to permit an easier birth. Her help extended beyond the delivery room. When a family called for Mary Ann to help, she might arrive with vegetables from her husband's garden, furniture, clothes and other items the family needed. In 1942, Mary Ann died as she lived, in service to others. On her way to a birth in a truck loaded with furniture and boxes full of useful items, Mary Ann took the only seat open on a rocking chair that was to be a gift for the family. She fell off the chair and onto the road. She died of injuries sustained in the accident.

70 Beekman St.

⑰ 61 ASH ST.
c. 1900 Vernacular
This building is much larger in size and scale than the buildings that surround it. It is generally believed that in the 1920s this building was used for bootlegging. The interior of the garage is spacious, with few vertical posts, so that large trucks could pull all the way into the garage. Of particular note is the rusticated stone on the garage.

⑱ 68 BEEKMAN ST.
c. 1870s Victorian Vernacular
In 1910, Alphonse DeRossi opened his restaurant here. DeRossi's was one of several restaurants in this area; others included DiGregorio's and Fusco's, that located at the same intersection of Beekman and Oak streets. This was a time when neighborhood groceries and restaurants flourished in the close-knit West Side community. The two-story open porches on this building set up a visual rhythm that unifies the architecture on the east side of Beekman Street.

⑲ 70 BEEKMAN ST.
c. 1880s
In the 1930s, the DeGregorio family owned this building. The family lived upstairs and operated a restaurant downstairs. This building, along with the other restaurants at the intersection of Beekman and Oak, were painted in white or light colors with adorning flower boxes creating a unique ambience. Today, the façade of the building reflects a 1920s Craftsman style, rather than its origins as a Victorian vernacular building. After years of neglect and decay, 70 Beekman St. is once again a vital part of the commercial district. True to its history, the building includes a second-story apartment, and new shops and galleries on the ground level.

⑳ 79 BEEKMAN ST.
c. 1848 Greek Revival
This building has retained much of its architectural integrity as an example of the Greek Revival style. Along with 73 Beekman St.,

a pattern can be seen in the placement of these small houses that emerged after the Saratoga and Schenectady Railroad came to the city. In the early 1880s, Foster Curtis, a carpenter, was the owner. It is probably during this period that the beautifully detailed Victorian Gothic porch was added. In 1893, the city directory lists Addison Curtis, a bookkeeper at Citizen's National Bank, as owner. Mr. Curtis lived here until 1896, when he moved to a house designed by R. Newton Brezee on Marion Place.

㉑ 73 BEEKMAN ST.

c. 1845 Greek Revival

This building represents the size and pattern of Greek Revival residences that were being built in this area in the 1840s and 1850s. One of the early owners was Daniel DeGroff, a carpenter, who lived in the house from 1868 to 1902. Beekman Street, along with lower Grand Avenue, grew with the railroad. A barbershop was built adjacent to the house in 1926, and is indicative of the commercial development of the street after 1900. Today, the barbershop has become an art gallery and the house provides studio space for artists.

㉒ 69 BEEKMAN ST.

c. 1845 Vernacular

Over the years, use of this building reflected the growth of Beekman Street from a quiet residential neighborhood to a commercial district

Beekman Street Arts District

42 Oak St.

after 1900. In 1868, Henry Freeman, a mason, made his home at 69 Beekman St. In 1900, Elmer Freeman opened a meat and vegetable market here. In the 1920s, Fusco's Restaurant opened; it operated there until the 1960s. Not long after, the Frederick Allen Lodge, an African- American fraternal organization, purchased the building, which has been greatly modified over the years. The building is essentially Greek Revival in design. The original structure had a low-pitch roof, with a gable front with pediment and dentil molding. The second-story porch was added later.

㉓ 13 OAK ST.
Principessa Elena Men's Society
The Principessa Elena Society was formed in 1890. This Italian men's club still exists today. The club promotes Italian heritage and brotherhood. St. Michael's Feast—honoring the patron saint of the West Side—has been held at the Principessa Elena Men's Society since 1914.

㉔ SO. FRANKLIN AT OAK STREET
Gideon Putnam Burying Ground
Gideon Putnam, responsible for the planning of Broadway and the first person to pipe Congress Spring, is laid to rest here. Putnam's contributions are visible throughout the city. Putnam gave the land for the burying ground to the city and was, ironically, the first person to be interred there. A stone wall, with an inset ironwork gate, surrounds the Putnam family plot. The headstones in the cemetery tell the story of the early development of the city. Also buried here are village leaders, hotel workers, tourists and soldiers. The Saratoga Springs Preservation Foundation restored the buring ground after years of vandalism threatened to destroy it.

RUTH,

Wife of
SAMUEL CHAPMAN
DIED DEC. 16,
1859,
AGED 6? YEARS

1 So. Franklin at Oak Street

NATIONAL MUSEUM OF DANCE
South Broadway
Washington Baths
1918-1920 Craftsman
attributed to Lewis F. Pilcher, architect

The National Museum of Dance is housed in the former Washington Baths, part of the Saratoga Spa State Park. The building is a wonderful example of the Craftsman style of architecture popular after World War I. Of particular note are the dormer windows above the entrance and the colonnaded porch spanning the front of the building, which is reminiscent of Gustav Stickley's designs. The two pergolas at the ends of the porch were once used as pleasant exterior spaces where patients could sit and enjoy the fresh air and are a significant architectural element of the building. The Washington Baths were built in the early development of the park and were part of an effort to create a world-class health resort there. The National Museum of Dance and Hall of Fame was established in 1986 and is the only museum in the nation dedicated to American professional dance. The museum houses a growing collection of photographs, videos, artifacts, costumes, biographies and archives that provide a contemporary and retrospective examination of seminal contributions to dance. The museum leases its historic building from the New York State Office of Parks, Recreation and Historic Preservation.

TANG TEACHING MUSEUM AND ART GALLERY
Skidmore College, North Broadway
2000, Post-Modern
Antoine Predock, architect

One of the few post-modern buildings in Saratoga Springs, the Tang Teaching Museum and Art Gallery, located in the center of the Skidmore College campus, reflects the interdisciplinary approach to the arts taught at the college. Rising from a hillside, surrounded by white pine trees, the angular, multi-level steel and glass structure has an organic design. The focal point of the building is a masonry tower at its center. The Tang houses both permanent collections and temporary exhibits, along with classrooms.

WHITNEY POLO FIELDS
Denton Road

Polo has been played in Saratoga Springs since 1898; the Saratoga Polo Association is one of the four oldest clubs in the nation. For a period of time between 1933 and 1979, polo was not played as an organized sport in Saratoga Springs. In 1978, the Whitney Polo Fields were rediscovered and the site was cultivated as playing fields once again. The fields are named for Harry Payne Whitney, an outstanding polo player, benefactor of the Saratoga Polo Association and a son of William Collins Whitney who helped develop the Saratoga Race Course. The Whitney Polo Fields are comprised of two playing fields, stables, a clubhouse, and pavilions. Matches are held from May through September.

SARATOGA SPA STATE PARK
South Broadway
1929-1934, Beaux-Arts
Joseph Henry Freedlander, architect
A.F. Brinkerhoff, landscape architect

The Saratoga Spa State Park, which was first named the New York State Reservation at Saratoga Springs, is an 800-acre park that was established as a result of legislation protecting the springs as a resource for the people of the state of New York. When Franklin Delano Roosevelt was governor of New York, he made the development of a world-class health resort in Saratoga Springs a priority for his administration. He commissioned an architect to study the great health resorts of Europe and to use this research to develop plans for the spa at Saratoga Springs. It was during FDR's presidency that the building program was funded as part of a government loan program — a precursor to the Work Projects Administration (WPA) program. Among the park's many attractions are a collection of impressive Beaux-Arts buildings, including the Administration Building, the Victoria Pool, the Roosevelt Bath Houses and the Hall of Springs. A hallmark of the design of the buildings is the strict symmetry of the facades. Moving out from the central entrance, a colonnaded porch with rounded arches spans the front terminating in a square pavilion at each end. In the pediments above the entrances to the Administration Building and the Hall of Springs, notice the statues of figures from Greek mythology. The classically styled buildings are set along intersecting malls that meet at a flagpole, similar in form to the mall in Washington D.C.

INDEX

JOIN
The Saratoga Springs Preservation Foundation
TODAY!

Since 1977, the Preservation Foundation has been the leading advocate of preserving and protecting the architectural, cultural and landscaped heritage of Saratoga Springs. Today, our focus continues to shine the spotlight on new opportunities for community growth through preservation, identifying endangered buildings threatened by neglect, and providing educational programming and technical assistance to homeowners and the community.

Your membership will support our ongoing programs and services to preserve Saratoga Springs.

Benefits of membership for individuals and/or couples....

$35 CONSERVATOR
❀ One-year subscription to Spirit of Preservation Newsletter
❀ Advance notice and discounts to events such as the Annual Fall and Candlelight House Tours
❀ Invitation to the Annual Meeting
❀ Listing in the Annual Report
❀ E-mail Alerts
❀ Free use of Foundation library resources

$75 LANDMARK
❀ All of the above, plus a premium gift (mug, tote or poster) and one complimentary Fall House Tour ticket

$150 EMPIRE
❀ All of the above, plus one complimentary pass to the Preservation Conference

$250 GOTHIC
❀ All of the above, plus one invitation to two stewardship events per year

$500+ BEAUX ARTS
❀ All of the above, plus one invitation to two preservation roundtables per year

Make a difference in the community and invest in YOUR Saratoga Springs!

☐   Yes, I would like to invest in Saratoga Springs with a membership to the Preservation Foundation.

☐   I am already a member, and I would like to gift a membership.

Please enroll me at the following level:

☐ $35 Conservator

☐ $75 Landmark

☐ $150 Empire

☐ $250 Gothic

☐ $500 Beaux Arts

For Landmark members and above, please check the free gift you would like to receive:

☐ TOTE   ☐ POSTER   ☐ MUG

Name_____

Address_____

_____

_____

Phone_____

E-mail_____

Method of Payment:

☐ Check   ☐ MasterCard   ☐ Visa   ☐ American Express

Credit Card #_____

Expiration Date_____

Signature_____

☐ I am interested in volunteering! Please contact me.

Annual membership and donations are tax deductible to the extent allowed by law.
Please make checks payable to Saratoga Springs Preservation Foundation.

Saratoga Springs Preservation Foundation
117 Grand Ave.
Saratoga Springs, NY 12866
www.saratogapreservation.org
(518) 587-5030

Sponsors

FRIENDS OF
THE BECKERMAN ARCHIVE

✳

Prudential Manor Homes
Norman M. Fox
and
Harvey & Kassie Fox
Realty USA
XPO Enterprises, LLC
(www.xpoenterprises.com)

FRIENDS OF *HOOFING IT!*

✳

Roohan Realty
Witt Construction

SUPPORTERS

✳

Barbara Glaser
Gallery 100
Edgar Woerner
70 Beekman Street Fine Art Gallery

✳

MEMBERS of the 2004-2005

The Saratoga Springs Preservation Foundation is funded in part
by a grant from the New York State Council of the Arts.